TRANSFORMING ABUSE

The greatest challenge of the day is:
how to bring about a revolution of the heart,
a revolution which has to start
with each one of us.

Dorothy Day

TRANSFORMING ABUSE

NONVIOLENT RESISTANCE AND RECOVERY

K. LOUISE SCHMIDT

NEW SOCIETY PUBLISHERS

Gabriola Island, BC   Philadelphia, PA

Canadian Cataloguing in Publication Data
Schmidt, K. Louise (Karen), 1956-
  Transforming Abuse

Includes bibliographical references,
ISBN 1-55092-258-0 -(bound) — ISBN 1-55092-259-9 (pbk.)
1. Women--Crimes against. 2. Child abuse. 3. Nonviolence. 4. Violence--
Moral and ethical aspects. I. Title.
HV6250.4.W65S35 1995   364.1'555   C95-910323-6

Cover design by Val Speidel.

Book design and typesetting by Consensus Communications,
Gabriola Island, BC.

Inquiries regarding requests to reprint all or part of *Transforming Abuse:
Nonviolent Resistance and Recovery* should be addressed to:

New Society Publishers,
P.O. Box 189, Gabriola Island, B.C., Canada V0R 1X0,
or
4527 Springfield Avenue, Philadelphia PA, U.S.A. 19143.

Canada ISBN: 1-55092-259-9 (Paperback)
Canada ISBN: 1-55092-258-0 (Hardback)
USA ISBN: 0-86571-314-6 (Paperback)
USA ISBN: 0-86571-313-8 (Hardback)

Printed in Berlin, Vermont on partially recycled paper using soy-based
ink by Capital City Press.

To order directly from the publishers, please add $3.00 to the price of the
first copy, and $1.00 for each additional copy (plus GST in Canada). Send
check or money order to:

New Society Publishers,
P.O. Box 189, Gabriola Island, B.C. Canada V0R 1X0
or
4527 Springfield Avenue, Philadelphia PA, U.S.A. 19143.

New Society Publishers is a project of the Catalyst Education Society, a
nonprofit educational society in Canada, and the New Society Educational
Foundation, a nonprofit, tax-exempt public foundation in the U.S. Opinions
expressed in this book do not necessarily reflect positions of the Catalyst
Education Society nor the New Society Educational Foundation.

To the wholeness of our beings.

TABLE OF CONTENTS

OUR WORK

ACKNOWLEDGMENTS

The writing of this book occured in two phases and places. The first version, called *To Live in Peace*, began as a nonviolence handbook for families and communities while I lived in Kaslo, British Columbia. I am grateful to Jack and Dottie Ross for welcoming me to the Nonviolence Resource Centre when I first arrived in Kaslo and speaking the responsibility they felt in securing feminist resources on nonviolence. *To Live in Peace* was published by the Argenta Friends Press and was made possible by a grant through the B.C. Ministry of Women's Equality and Carole Scott's advocacy. The Argenta Religious Society of Friends Monthly Meeting graciously administered the grant and created a community of care that provided spiritual and practical support for that project. My thanks to Jane Ballantyne, Bruce Farley, Mary Farley, Jay Martell, Shelley Stickle-Miles, Dottie Ross, Jack Ross, Marguerite and Jack Wells. Special thanks to Sylvia Raine whose care and conversation have been essential to the writing of *Transforming Abuse*.

I was invited to explore publicly some of the ideas included in *Transforming Abuse* in a community course on nonviolence in Kaslo in 1991. Thank-you to the Kootenay community who participated whole-heartedly and brought their wisdom to the fire. The Heart-Sharing Group, Marilyn Wolovick, Rich Claxton, Deborah Holmberg-Schwartz, Ron Schwartz and Beth McClellan, were particulary helpful during this stage of the journey.

In 1993, I moved to Gabriola Island, finished *To Live in Peace* and the following year began the rewrite that became *Transforming Abuse*. I am very grateful to those who were so generous with hospitality, friendship and assistance. Michael Candler, Leigh Ann Milman, Timothy Mika, Deborah Ferens, Cheryl McNeil, Alan Wilson, Brenda Gaertner and Howard Stiff made this transition possible in their rich sharing of gardens, meals, books and support. The Gabriola Women's Writer's Group provided inspiration and sanctuary when I was starved for the company of other writers. The Nanaimo Nonviolence Society provided and continues to offer opportunities for realizing and evolving the perspectives offered in this book. Thank-you all.

I am thankful for David Somerville and Judy Webb in Merville who welcomed me into their lives and sweat lodge—their healing prayers and direct action help me deepen my own practises of nonviolence with better balance. I will always remember those relations who held me in their hearts during this time, particularly my parents Alice and Henry Schmidt, Susan Mann, John McNamer and Christine Watt.

It is a privilege to experience publishers who take a Gandhian approach of stewardship with their authors. I have benefited from New Society's care and example, especially Judith Plant for her editing, warmth and willingness to stand by the book, and Christopher Plant for beginning the process and, later, for layout/design work. Others who contributed to the birth of Transforming Abuse include Anne Champagne who provided the copy-editing, Val Speidel who designed the cover, Alan Wilson who committed to layout and design for both phases of the book, and Ellen Bass for her wisdom. Any errors are my own and not the publishers'.

I am indebted to all the voices that have entered this text—the many writers and visionaries who devote their lives, persistently and passionately, to declaring a way without violence. I have learned and borrowed shamelessly from these visible teachers as I have from those not so visible—often women, the unpaid and unseen nonviolence activists who volunteer in shelters, crisis lines, on community boards, in coalitions and who are lightning rods for thousands of others.

I bow deeply to all my teachers of nonduality and interdependence. I am daily grateful for the Precepts of the Tiep Hien Order and the Buddhist nonviolence teacher and poet, Thich Nhat Hahn, for bringing these teachings in an unplanned appointment with his writing in 1987. I welcome the invitation to embody such love in action.

And, lastly, my gratitude to my friend Joanne Thorvaldson who midwifed Transforming Abuse despite the geographical difference in our lives. She is a stunning poet who found ways of holding the possibility of apples growing in the orchard when, to me, in times of despair, even the imagining of a blossom seemed impossible. For Joanne, the smallness and bigness of things are equal and, at some point, unimportant. She accompanied all my labor with great faith.

I bow to my sangha, this beautiful Earth.

K. Schmidt
Gabriola Island, 1995

FOREWORD

Ellen Bass

When my first child was born, I was immediately and overwhelmingly plunged into a kind of love that changed me in relationship to the world. Suddenly I cared about what became of the Earth and all its inhabitants in a way that was immeasurably more compelling than anything I'd ever felt before. I was flooded with love, and with it, anger. I wanted the world to be safe for my child. I wanted that more than I'd ever imagined I could want anything. And it wasn't safe. I was terrified and I was angry. These emotions were inextricably intertwined. And they motivated me to work toward making the world a safer place.

I welcome the publication of *Transforming Abuse: Nonviolent Resistance and Recovery* because it is rooted in a way of thinking that recognizes the compatibility—the deep connectedness—of ideas which have too often been seen as opposites.

As an outspoken advocate for the legitimacy of all feelings, including anger, I have sometimes been blamed for promoting hatred and revenge. They have asked how anyone can heal without forgiving the abuser, how survivors of abuse can be at peace if they're still angry or how they can come to resolution without reconciliation. In many people's minds there is no appreciation for—or even definition of—healthy anger. There is little understanding of one's rights—even responsibility—to protect oneself from further abuse. And an almost total incapacity to conceive of a state of being in which one is both angry and nonviolent, in which one protects onself without negating the humanity of another.

Most of us have been taught misleading information about anger. We have been taught to fear anger. We have been taught that it is dangerous, a sin, something to rise above, the opposite of love. In truth, anger and love are not incompatible. Sometimes, it is not until we truly love that we even care enough to be angry.

Dr. Bernice Reagon of the music group *Sweet Honey in the Rock* has expressed this union of love and anger in describing civil rights activist Fannie Lou Hamer as a "fierce warrior." She said, "I really like the feeling that in the midst of the most intense danger, there could be a sense of peace and safety. That you really could speak with immense anger about a situation and what people listening to you felt was how much love you had in you. Those are not lessons you get often. She was always so clear and so strong and insistent. And she was so mad and so loving."*

In my work with survivors of child sexual abuse, I talk about the distinction between anger and violence. Many of us are afraid of anger because we think it means violence—and we may have been victimized by that violence in our own families. But anger need not be violent. It is a feeling—and feelings do not damage or destroy. Violence is an action. It is one way to express anger, but not the only way. Violence is dangerous and destructive. None of us has the right to be violent, but we all have the right to our feelings.

Often people who were not abused as children challenge survivors' anger. They suggest that it would be better for the survivor if she—or he—weren't angry. Or, at best, that anger should be a stage of healing that one should strive to surpass. That forgiveness is a more evolved state than anger. And you're "more healed" if you forgive than if you don't. They suggest that the survivor extend compassion to the abuser.

In reality, the opposite of anger is rarely compassion. That opposite of anger is self-hatred. Anger is a natural response to violation. When that response is stifled, what results is anger turned against the self. As Adrienne Rich writes: "Most women have not even been able to touch this anger, except to drive it inward like a rusted nail."**

It is essential that we affirm every person's right to her or his authentic feelings. Feelings are not right or wrong. They are valuable resources, meaningful in themselves and essential teachers on our journey toward creating healthier selves and a healthier world.

I value the perspective of *Transforming Abuse* because it affirms the interrelatedness of anger and love, of feminism and nonviolence, of setting boundaries and forging alliances, asserting one's own rights and respecting the rights of others, self-care and caring for others. It embodies a strong, protective, respectful stance that we will not allow the abuse of children, of women, or of our Earth to continue unchecked. We take this stance not out of a desire for violence or revenge, but out of love.

*   From an interview with Bill Moyers.
** Adrienne Rich, "Disloyal to Civilization," in *Lies, Secrets, and Silence* (New York: W.W. Norton, 1979), p.309.

INTRODUCTION

We lay down the road in the walking

In this book, I see my task as "raising the grain" of nonviolent alternatives in our thinking about responses to male violence against women and children. I raise this grain by offering a process of questioning and listening. Thus, *Transforming Abuse* is not a step-by-step process of developing strategies. It is an invitation to look at principles of living that feed the psyche and to engage in a process of deepening awareness, action and healing.

The philosophies and practises of feminism and nonviolence show how issues of violence and recovery are related. Feminism opened an analysis of the oppression of women and children that revolutionized the movement toward social justice and made it more possible to imagine a nonviolent world. Nonviolence training gives us the tools to make this possible. The combined history of feminism and nonviolence has created alternatives to violence that build on the mutuality and equity of our human experiences.

THE QUESTIONS WE HAVE OF THE JOURNEY CHANGE RADICALLY AT POINTS ALONG THE WAY, AND YET THEY ARE STILL THE BASIC FUEL THAT DRIVES US FORWARD.
—CHRISTINA BALDWIN

Feminism and nonviolence respond to that which destroys and that which heals. They point the way to truth, justice and love. In this book, a feminist perspective of violence against women provides the politic behind the inquiry; a nonviolence perspective of transformation provides the spirit behind the alternatives. Feminism gives us the glasses, nonviolence gives us the eyes. Without feminism it is difficult to see the whole picture clearly. Without nonviolence we cannot transform the picture. Together, they are the necessary tools for personal and social change that is dynamically active in building respect for one another and resistance to violence.

The grain that is defining this work is still growing. As Jack Ross wrote: *There is no definition of nonviolence that suits everyone. This is as it should be: no great idea is capable of simple definition—try to get an agreement on "God" or "Love" for example.*[1] For the purpose of this book, I have defined nonviolence as *the mutual strengthening of relationship free from forms of physical, psychological, sexual or economic oppression.* This definition is mothered by a feminist vision of a just world for all.

I do not wish to impose another form of authoritative prerogative that does not spring from deep inside. So, in many ways, this book is a request to look into your hearts, see what you find there and proceed actively from there. I am learning along with you to unlearn doctrines of domination and subordination, the arrogance of absolutes and righteousness and, as I learn, I often think of Joan Halifax's reminder: *We lay down the road in the walking.*[2]

> I AM CERTAIN OF NOTHING BUT THE HOLINESS OF THE HEART'S AFFECTIONS AND THE TRUTH OF THE IMAGINATION.
> —*JOHN KEATS*

Its contents

Peaceful approaches to unrest in our lives require both reflection and action, solitude and support. Living peacefully is a process of helping ourselves so we are in a better position to help others. By developing hearts free from prejudice and an inner resolve not to harm ourselves or others, we are better able to transform problems in our lives. *Transforming Abuse* is designed as an introduction to nonviolence that can be explored on one's own or with others. This book offers approaches that can deepen hearing, thinking and resolution of nonviolent strength. We can begin by reaching into ourselves and by reaching out to those close to us.

Transforming Abuse is written in three parts. Part one, *Our Lives*, introduces the issues of violence against women and children and an overview of a feminist response located in the tradition of nonviolence. *Our Lives* provides a framework for part two, *Our Work*. *Our Work* is divided into eight chapters. Each chapter reflects an issue central to personal and community recovery of nonviolence. These eight topics are introduced in a five-to twleve-page synopsis designed for inquiry and reflection. Part three, *Our Future*, serves to further reflection on how we might approach nonviolent change in our lives. It suggests we broaden personal action into forms of creative justice based on deep democracy.

> THE PROBLEMS OF THE HUMAN HEART MUST FIRST BE SOLVED.
> —*THE DALAI LAMA*

Revolution of the heart

The revolution that will move us to justice and liberty is one that begins in the heart. It is this revolution that opens the way to nonviolence. This is a revolution whose wheels turn, daily and

2

enduringly, like the very Earth that holds us. It is observed in those citizens who, devoted to spiritual and political health, have turned toward the reformation of self, community, family and society. We are all needed to preserve the integrity and beauty of the living processes that link us one to the other. We are all needed as reformers recovering the depth and possibility of human care in the midst of great suffering.

ALTHOUGH THE WORLD IS FULL OF SUFFERING, IT IS ALSO FULL OF THE OVERCOMING OF IT.
—HELEN KELLER

A revolution that springs from the heart is one possessed by or propelled toward the possibility of unmitigated joy in the world. The joy that is possible when we engage in relieving suffering and affirming human dignity is boundless. When we are numb to the suffering in the world we also become closed to the joy that is possible when we transform suffering. The immense suffering experienced and witnessed in all the world's nations, including that of women and children abused by men, is a cry for direct action—for engagement in reform of the world.

No system, left or right, can solve the problems of today. There is a fundamentalism and corruption at large today, attached to profit, that is disconnected from spiritual and political health. We see the corruption in international commerce, international media and the patriarchal systems of old nation-states. This power is not viable. The enemies around us are also within—enemies whose power we must openly and honestly deconstruct, befriend and transform if we are to disarm violence in human relationships.

JOY IN THE JOY OF OTHERS IS A QUALITY WE TEND TO OVERLOOK. IT IS THE FLIPSIDE OF COMPASSION, AND TO THE EXTENT THAT YOU CAN EXPERIENCE THE SUFFERING OF ANOTHER AS YOUR OWN, YOU CAN ALSO EXPERIENCE THE JOY AND POWER AND GIFTS OF ANOTHER AS YOUR OWN.
—JOANNA MACY

There are as many minority supremacist governments within us as there are in our politico-economic infrastructures. We are all called to resist a morality developed out of a mindset of repression and subjugation and embrace an ethic of living devoted to cherishing differences, taking responsibility, and running boldly, even uncertainly, with the vision that each of us can peacefully lead lives of dignity. We must learn, with ourselves and those closest to us, an ethic of refusing hatred. Can we resist another decade of tyranny and reach into the next millennia with a joyful imperative? An imperative that lends itself to inventiveness, generosity, multiplicity, and even love?

We are a people and a society bent on a suicidal course of habit and denial, yet the potential for creating societies of justice and families of peace is monumental. It is only waiting for us to step forward and begin, and begin again. A revolution of relationships is taking place as the dominator paradigm—the one responsible for violence against one another—is collapsing. This is a revolution within families, spiritual traditions and societies that is changing radically how we communicate, make decisions, share resources, deepen consciousness and create choices.

THE WORLD IS ON FIRE. WE ARE IN DANGER. THERE IS ONLY TIME TO MOVE SLOWLY. THERE IS ONLY TIME TO LOVE.

—DEENA METZGER

Loving what is foreign

Resisting violence and recovering joy in our lives is not a one-way path. An abuser acts violently when he rejects aspects of himself that he has projected onto his victim. He tries to repress what he feels to be foreign, the other—woman and all he and society have projected onto her: tenderness, nurturing, dependence, weakness.... Each of us can make a difference by learning how to love and speak about what is most foreign in our lives, by taking back what has been dispossessed and finding a language that truly describes our reality. We must recognize that we all, in some small or large way, suffer from a spiritual exile of self from other and individual from community. We are all wounded and wanting for a love that does not annihilate.

THE POETIC WOULD BE THAT WHICH HAS NOT BECOME LAW.

—JULIA KRISTEVA

From the centuries-long void of women's voices I know there is a way of seeing, speaking and acting too long held in check. For myself, its recovery is a process of regaining a politic that does not refuse the poetic—sometimes defined as soul; sometimes as many systems working together, or synergy; sometimes as a celebration of diversity, pluralism or our interconnectedness; and sometimes, simply as harmless love.

Binary or dualistic logic sees the world in either/or terms: good or bad, strong or weak. Especially through the development of mechanized and scientific approaches to life, it has distilled human experience and voice into separate, compartmentalized units. Qualities that are considered male or female (such as assertiveness vs. co-operation) are polarized, the male given higher rank. When binary thinking places the differences between people within a paradigm for human relations of supremacy and subordination, the result is alienation and violence. Most of all I see this causes the human heart to harden or become machine-like—making it difficult for the heart to open and respond to suffering, unable to see and respect self as a changeable, exploratory and vulnerable being. Such a heart resists healing. We have been taught instead to guard our hearts and voices with an inner police state, an internal government based on dictatorship, strategy and tyranny. We live with a rigid, ungiving heart, a false democracy of self and language. We have been given life-depleting defence systems of many kinds to guard our lives, all sorts of arsenals to reproduce on an emotional level of existence a consciousness of warfare.

A non-binary logic is one that refuses to follow that which splits our body from our soul. It is knowing the internal vigilance necessary to create true sexual and economic democracy. It is the logic of the open heart—not the way of opposition or alienation, of either/or, us/them, mind over nature, but the way of interdependence. It is what Buddhist thought describes in the doctrine of *paticca samuppada* as dependent co-arising or deep relationship with the world through awareness of mutual causality. It is about love that is not born out of commerce or control but of relatedness, responsibility and respect.

WHEN WE LOOK DEEPLY, WE FIND THERE ARE NO SEPARATE REALITIES.
—JOAN HALIFAX

Descartes and all the other great colonizers of land, psyche, the cosmos, of race and women have shown us their fear of the unknown, out of which has developed conquests of catastrophic destruction including an insane attempt to conquer time and life itself. The sickness of conquest is a patriarchal mindset that shows us, terribly, where we need to go. We need to build an ethic of living that is decolonized, which refuses exploitative ownership and control of any kind. We need to approach the unknown places, the foreign places in ourselves and our culture with a willingness to bring safety, understanding and healing. We need to find a way of seeing and hearing and speaking that does not dispossess a person of their reality, feelings, words or dreams.

A non-enemy ethic

Nonviolence is defining for myself the life I want and refusing to build any relationship—erotic, economic, religious, parental or social—based on control or exploitation of another. My defining of personal and global change needs to be life-affirming. Or as Adrienne Rich said, *If it doesn't smell like the earth, it isn't good for the earth.*[3] I want the ethics of my life to smell like the earth. For myself this is a feminist way of living that means a few things. I want my inner nature to be in deep relationship with the natural laws of this planet. I want to live my life with dignity and peace. I want to keep reaching for relationship that strengthens this possibility while resisting relationship based on domination. An ethic of resisting and reaching, of simultaneously rejecting dehumanizing behavior

WE ARE NOT ENEMIES OF ONE ANOTHER—OUR REAL ENEMIES ARE HUNGER, DISEASE, RACISM, POVERTY, INEQUALITY, INJUSTICE AND VIOLENCE.
—WOMEN FOR A MEANINGFUL SUMMIT

while respecting the dignity due us all, is what traditional nonviolence theory calls a two-handed approach or *moral ju-jitsu*. A double gesture of refusing violence while reaching out to the suffering is a decentralization of power.

This requires me to live my life from an ethic that is non-enemy-based, developing a non-enemy consciousness that begins first with myself, with self-respect. I am not my worst enemy. I can be in respectful relationship to this planet, despite all odds. I live from the principle that I have the right to live without bodily and psychological assault, that we all do. I know that when one person suffers, we all do. This kind of consciousness has awakened me to the profound reality that, as Barbara Deming and activists before her put it, *we are all part of one another.* We are meant to co-exist.

So it doesn't help to try to eradicate problems by seeing others as my enemies and putting the blame always outside, over there, with them. An abused woman is not helped by seeing her attacker only as the enemy, and an abuser feeds his violence by seeing the woman he's assaulting as the problem. A non-enemy ethic means I am part of the story as well as the solutions. It is the desire for what Buddhists call *Bahu syam prajayera* or the will to become many hearts. In this light, more than anything, nonviolent activism has taught me that we are undeniably linked and responsible for the link that we inherit at our birth.

Our relatedness is what is most precious and everything we think, say and do affects one another. There are many traditions that honor this relatedness. People who practice deep ecology, the way of an undivided heart, reclamation of wholeness, and social action are all around us. When we understand our relatedness, we can stop violence against all our relations, human and otherwise, and choose instead mindful growth, wholeness, gratitude and reciprocity. *Vengeance*, Barbara Deming wrote, *is not the point. Change is.*[4]

Inner and outer coups

For me this calls for both inner and outer coups: subversive acts that overturn and leap out of states of self- and state-imposed dictatorship. I do this by participating in both inner and outer change that affects the spiritual and political, private and public, familial and social, scientific and poetic spheres of my life. The coups are often outbursts from prisons of silence, marginalization and domination; out of systems and ideologies of violence, death and supremacy. They involve recognizing the places of dichotomy in my own life, the divisionary thinking and polarizations that destroy mutual strengthening of relationship. If I want simplicity and wiser use of resources then I must live more simply and consume less. If I want peace in my life, then I must practise peaceful ways of living.

If we are to break the psychology of physical and sexual abuse, we must all become law breakers: people who refuse to live from a logic designed to separate our differences into hierarchical compartments controlled by a fanaticism of superiority, fear, hatred and greed. We are all called to find creative ways of refusing laws based on domination and exploitation, and our resistance, if it is in decades to come to transform a rape culture, must be nonviolent. Each of us can make a difference by learning how the dominant systems in our world enforce alienation from our deepest selves. We can look at how our creative capacities are limited by mechanized and detached thinking and instead, learn to affirm the diversity and dignity of human lives. *The truth, above all*, Barbara Deming wrote, *is that every human being deserves respect. By actively practising nonviolence, we assert the respect due ourselves, when it is denied, through non-co-operation; we assert the respect due all others, through our refusal to be violent.*[5]

Practising nonviolence calls for nothing less than subversion of the old laws of commerce and domination through a conspiracy of alliance and respect. I am not going to suppress something so simple as my desire for life and the right with others to protection of that life—a desire to live life from within, from the locality of this body, this place and time, in as whole and connected a way as I can. I am looking for transformation based on care and justice, alliance and complementarity. Building new systems is work I need to do very carefully, and very gently. And I have learned the simpler the effort the more possible it is. So I am trying to make the ethics that govern my life less complicated and the tasks more focused.

IT IS IN THE KNOWLEDGE OF THE GENUINE CONDITIONS OF OUR LIVES THAT WE MUST DRAW OUR STRENGTH TO LIVE AND OUR REASONS FOR ACTING.
—*SIMONE DE BEAUVOIR*

IT'S NOT IMPOSSIBLE, AND THIS IS WHAT NOURISHES LIFE—A LOVE THAT HAS NO COMMERCE.
—*HÉLÈNE CIXOUS*

An ecology of self

Nonviolence is the only recovery path from violence I know of that works. Choosing to practise nonviolence (for it is a practice to continue to face the fear and violence in my life, a daily practice) can mean paying attention to privilege and how I use resources;

7

what and how I eat and drink; what work I choose; how I work; where and how I get my food; how I relate to children and elders; how I treat plants, animals and the ecosystem; how I rest, listen, and take time to give thanks. Here, nonviolence becomes a practice of balance, an ecology of self. To try to engage my spirit, mind and body equally in the world means I must work with my hands as well as with my intellect and heart. For balance to happen—to truly practise peaceful approaches to unrest—I find I require both reflection and action, solitude and support, speech and silence. The will to join hearts in a movement of peace, I am learning painfully slowly, is impossible without balance.

STUDY THE SELF.
—DOGEN

I believe we all suffer from divisionary and polarizing thinking, are all out of balance in different degrees at different times particularly because of win-lose ethics, from which in the long run everyone suffers. Developing a non-enemy ethic in my life means refusing to hate and refusing to win at a cost to others. I am trying to look for the human face behind the enemy image and in this find a possible transformation of relationship.

Turning the wheel

I find much of the work of nonviolence like gardening—a constant process of persistence and patience, upturning and supplanting, giving and receiving. There are rebellions in all gardens; in our unfolding there can always be new growth, ideas and capacities that transgress the landscape of violence that is so vivid in our minds and fixed in our culture. With mindful consideration of how we live on this planet we can find ways of transforming old ideologies and orders that sanction intentional harm. What decay we find in our gardens can eventually become food.

MY BUSINESS IS
CIRCUMFERENCE.
—EMILY DICKINSON

The development of nonviolence and the disarmament of violence requires the same attention as the tomato seeds we might plant and seedlings we nurture. It is a daily and careful process. We never really know what our planting will bring. Gardens are not only linear processes; they are cyclical and circuitous. They circulate all sorts of unexpected energies and events. There are also all kinds of external conditions affecting the growth of any planting. Yet, if we can prevent ourselves from becoming rigid in our expectations and experimentation, and allow practices and principles of peace to guide our efforts, the outcome is bound to be fruitful.

Writing *Transforming Abuse* has allowed me to look directly at the absence and presence of courage, the beauty and beast of change. It has been an effort of not being fixed—a process sometimes very painful and other times, unexpectedly joyous. I have attempted to hold the tension so often experienced in the confusion and calamity caused by violence and in this holding, embody an approach to nonviolent resistance and recovery that is fluid and dynamic. I am seeking freedom from internal and external tyranny, and looking for many possibilities in this crossing. This crossing is a continual revolution of attitude and action.

WE ARE TENDER, GROWING THINGS AND THE SHAPES OF OUR BODIES MAP OUT THE WORLD.
—JOANNE THORVALDSON

I find at times I encounter a pathological doubt about the possibility of transformation—our ability to turn the wheel in another direction. I believe this doubt exists in many forms in our lives. The problem of not believing in the practice and possibility of peace is paramount and has pushed me to ask myself and others: Are we not all called to build confidence in our basic and true natures—the inherent harmless wholeness residing in each of us? Are we not all called to refuse to abandon ourselves and others when we are challenged by the rampant warfare pathology of hate, secrecy and fear that only violence can propagate? Are we willing to stop our own acts of complicity each time we blame a victim and absolve an abuser?

We have woundedness and health. There is a bridge between the two and when I am willing to walk it, I find a way forward. We can walk this bridge together and build communities of healing where the wounded and wounder are both provided for. In my life this bridge is being built inside and out. Personal liberation and social responsibility are inextricably intertwined; they are two plants of the same garden. Unless the social conditions that create a culture of violence are understood and changed, our work toward a goal of peace will be endless. And unless the seeds of peace are planted in our very souls, our dream of the other becoming a friend will not be realized.

I AM THE WOMAN/ OFFERING TWO FLOWERS/ WHOSE ROOTS ARE TWIN JUSTICE AND HOPE/ LET US BEGIN.
—ALICE WALKER

I am learning I cannot forsake the inside for the outside or the outside for the inside. The bridge between the two, the spiritual and the political, intention and action, is the way. Please help me walk this bridge with nonviolent steps. If we put many shoulders to the wheel turning us toward peace then our joy will be great.

Peaceful self-governance

I GO WHERE I LOVE
AND WHERE I AM
LOVED,/
INTO THE SNOW;/
I GO TO THE
THINGS I LOVE/
WITH NO THOUGHT
OF DUTY OR PITY.

—H.D.

I write as an observer, a witness. My own story walks alongside the observations and the voices of others I have included here. My story is the visibility of the life I lead, sometimes clumsy but also steadily strengthening. At my worst, I repeat the same old tactics that divide us. At my best, I bring an honest effort to recovering respect and responsibility, sexuality and economy from institutional and multinational systems of governing and returning them to local governing. I start with this one—peaceful self-governance—and reach out from there.

The ideas, questions and resolutions proposed in *Transforming Abuse* are results of the spiritual inquiry and political action of myself and those around me who have helped create these perspectives, knowingly and unknowingly. *Transforming Abuse* may serve as an opening for some, a reminder for others. Hopefully, it will unsettle us enough to make us want to act where we are needed, to recover, or to continue with efforts of nonviolence, however small or large. I write from the conviction there is no one answer. It is closer to the truth to simply become more aware of and engaged in the choices we have. As Sharon Olds wrote to a friend, *all I can do is point out the two paths; we can go down either.*[6]

WHERE ONE'S
FOOT IS IS WHERE
TRUTH IS TO BE
FOUND.

—JOAN HALIFAX

Notes

[1] Jack Ross, *Nonviolence for Elfin Spirits* (Argenta, B.C.: Argenta Friends Press, 1992), p. 73.

[2] Joan Halifax, "The Road is Your Footsteps," in Thich Nhat Hahn et al., *For a Future to Be Possible: Commentaries on the Five Wonderful Precepts* (Parallax Press, 1993), p. 47. In this essay Joan Halifax enlivens Antonio Machado's original poem and reminder.

[3] Adrienne Rich, *Blood, Bread and Poetry* (New York: W.W. Norton & Company, 1986), p. 14.

[4] Barbara Deming, *We Are All Part of One Another*, ed. Jane Meyerding (Philadelphia & Gabriola Island: New Society Publishers, 1984).

[5] Ibid., p. 211.

[6] Sharon Olds, "When," in *Women on War: Essential Voice for the Nuclear Age*, ed. Daniela Gioseffi (New York: Touchstone, 1988), p. 244.

OUR LIVES

I VIOLENCE AGAINST WOMEN AND CHILDREN

1. The sexuality of terrorism

The list of human rights violations against women and children is unending. Violence against women is the most pervasive human rights issue in the world. Amnesty International reports violations continue to occur "in every region of the world and under every system of government."[1] The violation of women's human rights through abuses, exploitation, discrimination and murder constitutes a civil emergency in every country of this planet.

Organized violence is widely practised historically, as warfare and terrorism. In the 1970s, the battered women's movement brought to our attention that women's basic human rights were being violated in ways parallel to prisoners and hostages; indeed there are untold numbers of women who are held hostage in North American homes. Forms of brainwashing, ongoing coercion and physical violence are common experiences of abused women. Violence directed at women, whether in war or private relationships, is intended to break down the victim's body or psyche. Next to the military, the home has become the most violent institution in North America.

Today, there is an international lobby for the United Nations Human Rights Commission to adopt by consensus a resolution identifying rape of women as a war crime. This is in response to the 50,000 Croatian and Muslim women raped by Bosnian Serb soldiers as a systematic strategy of war. Dispatches from Bosnia and Herzegovina have included testimonies of young girls sexually enslaved and witness to others being slaughtered after mass rapes.[2] Social response to battered and raped women has historically been one of doubt and disbelief. In the way of response and reform, little has been done to make men who rape and batter accountable for these crimes.

The sexuality of terrorism brings its reality into our own communities. Our daily lives are full of images of sexuality and violence presented as the epitome of male power. The common norm of sex as violence and violence as sexy helps destroy clear thinking about the differences between pain and pleasure. More and more, men feel powerful in giving pain and as a gender class, women are often the target of the profound fear and hatred, brokenness and alienation experienced in our human race.

2. Pornography

A news report in Banja Luka, a Serb-occupied city in West Bosnia, showed Serbian tanks plastered with pornography, tanks carrying soldiers who were continuing the "ethnic cleansing" of non-Serbs. There were also televised rapes shown on the evening news—media terrorism that demonstrated how in this war "pornography emerges as a tool for genocide."[3] Catherine MacKinnon, in her article "Turning Rape into Pornography: Postmodern Genocide," does well to ask: "How does genocide become so explicitly sexually obsessed? How do real rapes become ordinary evening news?"[4]

The phenomenon of pornography as the industry we know today dates primarily from 1945, in the context of post-war masculinity packaged for the masses. Values associated with Hefner's *Playboy* of "being uncommitted to a relationship, expressing exuberant heterosexuality and making lots of money and not having to share with a wife or children" boosted the U.S. economy through white male exploitation of women.[5] Annual profits since the 1960s have increased from $5 million to $5 billion. Pornography exploits women and children, many of whom were sexually abused as children—"an experience," Rus Ervin Funk describes, "that concretely reinforces the notion that their value as human beings is based on their physical attractiveness and their willingness to be sexually pleasing and available to men."[6]

Pornographers in the U.S. are the largest exporters of pornography and the largest importers of women and children as commodities in the global sexual slavery industry.[7] Many of the imported sex slaves are Asian and "light-skinned" women of color. With pornography and prostitution defining the condition of these women and children, pornography introduces a modern slave trade that extends from a white colonialist mentality of entitlement and subordination. It is critical to understand the link between the

WHAT VIOLENCE MEANS TO A WOMAN CAN ONLY BE UNDERSTOOD IF SHE FEELS SAFE TO SPEAK HER OWN TRUTH, IMPOSSIBLE IN MALE-IDENTIFIED INSTITUTIONS SUCH AS THE JUDICIARY, THE UNIVERSITY, AND RELIGIOUS COLONIES.
—*NAIDA HYDE AND HELGA JACOBSON*

YES, IF MEN AND WOMEN—AND WOMEN AND WOMEN, AND MEN AND MEN—SHOULD FINALLY LEARN TO COME TOGETHER SIMPLY AS HUMAN BEINGS, NO MORE AND NO LESS, THEN LOVE WOULD NO LONGER DRAW WOMEN BACKWARD BY THE HAIR, AWAY FROM THEMSELVES; AND IT WOULD NO LONGER DRIVE MEN TO SEEK THEMSELVES WHERE THEY WILL NEVER FIND THEMSELVES, IN DESPOILING OTHERS, AND DESPOILING THE EARTH ITSELF.
—*BARBARA DEMING*

15

oppression of women and the role of slavery in shaping socio-economic patterns between race, class and sex.

The continuum of economic, reproductive and sexual exploitation runs sharply through all women's history. For many women, the idea of political or personal freedom is impossible as long as "male culture" perpetuates the colonialist doctrines of conquest and appropriation. In her essay "In Praise of Insubordination," Inés Hernandez-Avila writes, "I cannot imagine a world without rape without imagining a world not ruled by the logic of capitalism and imperialism which continues to justify subordination, dehumanization, and exploitation."[8] Andrea Dworkin told us more than a decade ago:

> If one sees how exploited women are—the systematic nature of the exploitation, the sexual base of the exploitation—then there is no political or ethical justification for doing one whit less than everything—using every resource—to stop that exploitation.[9]

MOREOVER, THE FEMALE BODY IS NOT ONLY ABUSED BUT EXPLOITED: WOMEN WORLDWIDE CONTRIBUTE 2/3 OF THE WORK HOURS, EARN 1/10 OF THE INCOME AND 1/100 OF THE PROPERTY.
—CHARLENE SPRETNAK

Dworkin's call for "a 24-hour truce during which there is no rape," which resounded in a speech given in 1983 at the U.S. Midwest Regional Conference of the National Organization for Changing Men, has yet to be realized. The organization of men against rape is minimal.

The misogyny and degradation involved as pornography links violence with sex and male power with women's subjugation is seen in the increasing amount of male violence in the wider entertainment business. Movies portraying women who are hounded, terrorized, slashed, raped and murdered are viewed by boys who will see an average of 250,000 acts of violence and 40,000 attempted murders on television before they are eighteen.[10] Researchers have shown that violent pornography (1) intensifies the predisposition of some men to rape—a predisposition that is already present in up to 60% of college-age young men; (2) undermines some men's internal inhibitions against acting out rape desires; (3) undermines social inhibitions against acting out rape desires; (4) reinforces several sexual assault myths; (5) desensitizes men and women to violence against women and children; and (6) is actually a *documentary* of coercion and sexual abuse.[11]

AND HERE I MUST STEP WARILY, FOR ALREADY I FEEL THE LASH UPON MY SHOULDER.
—VIRGINIA WOOLF

Aggressive pornography is central to the sexual obsession, control, hatred and detachment often associated with rape and forms of sexual coercion. Many violent men who are addicts to fantasies of control and domination fear the full humanity of intimacy and sexuality, and the gains women are making in freeing themselves from subordination. The commodification of women keeps this fear in check, rendering the joys of mutually affirming relationships with women very difficult, if not impossible. Pornography cannot affirm the worth of the user or those exploited.

Sex and images of sex are not the problem. The linking of sex with violence is a problem, particularly mass media representation of sexual violence. In *Not A Love Story: A Film About Pornography*, Kate Millet argued "that instead of embracing erotica we were hoodwinked into accepting pornography; the pornography industry burgeoned by manipulating a sincere desire for a less repressive sexuality into legitimization of an exploitative product."[12] The problem, Gloria Steinem writes, "is that there is so little erotica" and "so much pornography."[13]

Pornography is now a civil rights issue. In February 1992, Canada's Supreme Court established a precedent in North America that a threat to the equality and safety of women—the harm-to-women approach of the civil rights anti-pornography ordinance pioneered by Andrea Dworkin and Catherine MacKinnon—"is a substantial concern which justifies restricting the otherwise full exercise of the freedom of expression." It was ruled that "obscenity is to be defined by the harm it does to women and not by what offends our values": *Materials portraying women as a class of objects for sexual exploitation and abuse have a negative impact on the individual's sense of self-worth and acceptance.*[14] Censorship issues prevail, as does the reality that many women who have survived battering, rape, incest and attempted murder describe their abusers as pornography consumers and addicts, who in many cases would force them to act out scenes from films or poses in pictures.[15]

The link between pornography, militarism and rape is most obvious when we consider the dehumanization of another that is necessary before asserting the "right" to exploit or violate another. Sexual atrocities that are presaged through pro-rape pornography are the result of the same feelings and behaviors of control and dominance that are found in any practice of violence. For systemized rape to be finally recognized as a war crime and included in post-war indictments of documented forms of torture, the turning of rape into pornography will also have to be recognized. For rape of women and children to be considered as crimes and for these crimes to be more adequately brought to justice

AND THE LIE IS THAT MEN AND WOMEN ARE ALTOGETHER DIFFERENT, ONE FROM ANOTHER. AGAIN, A TRANSPARENT LIE. FOR HOW COULD IT BE SO—WHEN THE ONE IS MADE FROM THE VERY FLESH AND BLOOD OF THE OTHER? BUT AGAIN, IT IS INSISTED UPON. IT IS EVEN INSISTED UPON THAT THE MALE IS NOT REALLY BORN OF THE MOTHER. THE PATRIARCHAL CHURCH TEACHES: EVERYTHING REALLY "PROCEEDETH FROM THE FATHER AND THE SON." DO NOT ASK HOW. THE LIE AT THE VERY HEART OF MASCULINE PRIDE IS THIS: THAT THE MOTHER IS NOT REALLY THE MOTHER; THE MOTHER IS UNNECESSARY....

—BARBARA DEMING

in our "countries of peace," the impact of pornography on the male construction of sexuality and on rape will have to be recognized. Anytime we learn that "sex is violent and violence sexy," women and children are put in danger. It is as Anne Jones describes: "an intoxicating connection of violence and sex and tyranny that misguides "young males," and provides both a violent scenario and a sexy justification for the batterer, or indeed the average man."[16]

3. No one is immune

According to the 1993 Statistics Canada national survey on violence against women, one-half of all Canadian women have experienced at least one incident of violence since the age of 18. One million women a year are physically abused by their husbands or male partners. Many women who reported violence in a current marriage have at some point felt their lives were in danger. Women whose partners had witnessed violence by their fathers endured more severe and repeated violence than women whose fathers-in-law were not violent. Ninety-five per cent of the victims of spousal assault are women.

We lose lives through conjugal violence. An average of 13 wives and four husbands per million couples are killed each year in Canada. Over the period 1974-92, a married woman was nine times more likely to be killed by her spouse than by a stranger. An average of two women a week were killed by their husbands or male partners in 1990. Women are 75% more likely to be killed at the time they leave, separate from or divorce their partners.[17]

Ninety per cent of the victims of sexual assault in Canada are women. One Canadian woman out of every four will be sexually assaulted at some time in her life if the consciousness and practice of rape in our culture is not eradicated. Only one in ten assaults is ever reported to police, only one in 100 cases of date rape is reported.[18] In the U.S., the National Crime Victimization Survey (U.S. Survey of Consensus for the Bureau of Justice Statistics) reported 171,420 rapes for 1991—one rape every 3.5 minutes. The FBI Uniform Crime Report showed 106,593 rapes in 1991. Only 16% or one out of six rapes was ever reported to police. The true number of rapes in the U.S. each year is likely to be in the range of 639,500. At that rate over a 20-year period, there would be more than 12 million American women rape survivors. Yet, in the majority of sex crimes against women in North America, "women are put on trial as if they planned and executed their own rape."[19]

Children suffer the trauma of violence when they witness abuse of their mother or father or are victims themselves. In the U.S., the National Committee for Prevention of Child Abuse counted 404,100 reports of child sexual abuse by caretakers in its 1991 survey of child protective service agencies. These reports do not take into account sexual abuse by non-caretakers. More than three million children witness acts of domestic violence every year. Children of abused mothers are six times more likely to attempt suicide and 50% more likely to abuse drugs and alcohol. More than half of abused women who are mothers beat their children.[20] In two studies it was found that between 53 and 70% of men who battered their wives or girlfriends also abused a child; in households with four or more children it was found that 92% of the batterers of women also abused the children.[21] Over two-thirds of child victims of violent crimes are killed by a parent. In Canada, over 70% of victims were killed before they were five years old.[22]

Adolescent prostitutes and runaways, boys and girls, commonly come from a background of abuse. Victims of childhood abuse are at a much greater risk of becoming adult abusers. A clear statistical analysis of child abuse is difficult to assess as only extreme cases usually come to the attention of police and child protection workers. Many women do not feel safe enough to call police for fear of unsettling an already explosive situation, possibly leading to more violence after the police leave. Only in the last five years, largely because of the courage of First Nations men breaking the silence surrounding residential abuse, are we getting a clearer picture of what boys have experienced.

Women who leave abusive relationships may seek refuge in shelters or transition houses for battered women. Shelters across North America are often full and have difficulty accommodating the numbers of abused women needing refuge and counselling for themselves and their children. A minimum of 600,000 women a year are provided this service in Canada.[23]

Unless the criminal justice system is responsibly active and accountable for law enforcement programs, legislation regarding sentencing and re-education of abusive men accomplishes little. Protection of battered women and children and just prosecution of abusive men must be co-ordinated if it is to succeed. Change has

IT IS ORGANIZED VIOLENCE ON TOP WHICH CREATES VIOLENCE AT THE BOTTOM.
—EMMA GOLDMAN

THE CHILD SHALL BE PROTECTED AGAINST ALL FORMS OF NEGLECT, CRUELTY AND EXPLOITATION. [SHE OR HE] SHALL NOT BE THE SUBJECT OF TRAFFIC, OF ANY FORM.
—UN DECLARATION OF THE RIGHTS OF THE CHILD

been dangerously slow despite the picture that is getting clearer and clearer: no one is immune; abuse affects all our lives.

4. Surviving daily violence

The capacity of any traumatized person to free him- or herself from violence is reduced each day the abuse continues. Resistance, through force, in most situations is impossible. As Robin Morgan states, "If a woman who is being beaten fears striking back, it is because she knows, first, that he can come for her and kill her in retaliation, and, second, that if *she* kills in her own defense, then not he but his State will come for her. Women know that we cannot win by force—*that no one really can*—and therefore women seek to resolve problems by other means."[24] Women do resist though; and it is often because we resist that control over our lives is tightened by an abusing partner.

It has been well documented that the cycle of violence in most homes will, without intervention, increase over time in frequency and severity.[25] Anyone suffering emotional and physical injury is diminished in strength, decision-making skills and self-worth. Women often live or work in circumstances where they have to conceal injury, trauma and fear, lest they suffer public humiliation from those who scorn or diminish her situation or, as so often happens, lest they be blamed for the abuse and again humiliated. Numerous women also fear state appropriation of their children.

Many women who are unaware of their basic human rights or are unable to take the necessary action for their safety will look for ways of placating or accommodating their abuser. Energy needed to reach out for help and safety is often used in worrying about when the next violent episode will occur and how damages can be minimized. Moreover, when women do reach out and are refused sanctuary and service, the dangerous belief that nothing can be done is reinforced. Women who do leave their violent partners often face the possibility of losing their home. Many are harassed, stalked or kidnapped.

In abusive relationships, victims often become like hungry ghosts, psychically and physically. Domestic violence causes 30,000 emergency room visits and 100,000 days of hospitalization every year in the United States. In one of the most important books we have today documenting battering and recommending intervention, *Next Time She'll Be Dead*, Anne Jones describes the

I NEVER HEAR THE WORD "ESCAPE" WITHOUT A QUICKER BLOOD.
—EMILY DICKINSON

injuries incurred through battering:

> Untold numbers of women suffer permanent injuries—brain damage, blindness, deafness, speech loss through laryngeal damage, disfigurement, and mutilation, damage to or loss of internal organs, paralysis, sterility, and so on. Countless pregnant women miscarry as a result of beatings, and countless birth defects and abnormalities can be attributed to battery of the mother during pregnancy. So many battered women have been infected with HIV by batterers who force them into unprotected sex...that the National Centers for Disease Control have identified a direct link between battering and the spread of HIV and AIDS among women....
>
> After they escape, battered women may be saddled for years with a load of complicated problems ranging from anxiety, shame, and despair to flashbacks and suicidal ideation. These aftershocks are the symptoms of post-traumatic stress disorder, a psychological syndrome seen also in survivors of rape and incest and in veterans of wartime combat.[26]

THIS IS WHAT I AM: WATCHING THE SPIDER/ REBUILD— "PATIENTLY," THEY SAY, BUT I RECOGNIZE IN HER/ IMPATIENCE— MY OWN— THE PASSION TO MAKE AND MAKE AGAIN/ WHERE SUCH UNMAKING REIGNS THE REFUSAL TO BE A VICTIM/ WE HAVE LIVED WITH VIOLENCE SO LONG.
—ADRIENNE RICH

The magnitude of trauma suffered from psychological, physical and sexual violence is parallel to any form of warfare. In 1982, in her book *Rape in Marriage*, Diana Russell reprinted information from an Amnesty International Publication, *Report on Torture*. This report included the *Biderman's Chart of Coercion*, methods of brainwashing and control tactics used in war, documented by Alfred D. Biderman. These tactics, Russell and other women illustrated, have all been forms of abuse experienced in marriage by women. What is effective in concentration camps, it was shown, is also effective in enforcing power over another in domestic abusive relationships.

These forms of abuse include "gas-lighting" or "mind-bending" in which "men who have the cognitive aptitude and are adept at leaving no marks" employ invisible forms of violence that severely undermine a woman's reality through subtle forms of mind control or exploitation of "women in subgroups where oppression is still not seen as unacceptable" and these women have little chance of being believed.[27] All the methods of coercion documented by Alfred D. Biderman have been described by abused women—systematic isolation, monopolizing of perception, induced debility and exhaustion, threats, occasional indulgences, demonstrating omnipotence, degradation and the enforcement of trivial demands.[28]

PATRIARCHY IS A LONG WINTER.
—BARBARA DEMING

There is no measuring tool that tells us the magnitude of trauma survivors suffer. Anyone suffering from violence needs protection.

The brutality of everyday violence clearly calls to those of us not trapped in such a prison to confront violence in our communities and bring real care, education and justice to those in need, whether she or he be victim or violator, child or adult.

5. Accountability

Social silence around violence against women has built a deafening roar of denial. On a national level, one rapist in 20 is arrested, one out of 30 prosecuted, one out of 60 convicted. As Carol Adams says so clearly, *where there is denial, there is no call to accountability to the perpetrators of violence. In the absence of accountability, abuse continues.*[29] Criminal prosecution is the only way to establish that sexual and physical abuse are criminal activities. Without legal sanctions neither protection nor accountability is established. Any effective criminal justice program must charge and jail dangerous men. On a community level, changes in belief systems around issues of entitlement, responsibility and respect (for instance, that men are entitled to female compliance) need to permeate all personal and social change responses. Creative justice work can begin today in social discourse, education and family dynamics.

Haki R. Madhubuti, in his essay "On Becoming Anti-Rapist," writes:

> Male acculturation...is antifemale, antiwomanist/feminist, and antireason when it comes to women's equal measure and place in society. This flawed socialization of men is not confined to the West but permeates most, if not all, cultures in the modern world. Most men have been taught to treat, respond, listen, and react to women from a male's point of view.[30]

Madhubuti tells us that men are most often "imprisoned with an intellectual/spiritual/sexual understanding of women based on an antiquated male culture and sexist orientation."[31] Men need to learn to look to other men who are practising a humanity based on relating with dignity and care to one another and to women as equals. Unless our orientation to intimacy is one that seeks to support the full happiness and health of one another, then the preciousness and potential of each other's life is forgotten.

Rape and abuse will not stop until all human beings are allowed their full humanity. Peggy Miller and Nancy Biele, in their essay "Twenty Years Later: The Unfinished Revolution," write:

PERSONAL TRUTHTELLING AS A PATH TO SOCIAL CHANGE IS THE MOST IMPORTANT AND ENDURING LEGACY.
—GLORIA STEINEM

DIALOGUE CANNOT OCCUR BETWEEN THOSE WHO WANT TO NAME THE WORLD AND THOSE WHO DO NOT WANT THIS NAMING.
—PAULO FREIRE

Men rape because they can. Sexual violence is sanctioned, at worst, taught, and at best, excused. Once we believed that those who rape women and children had been harmed themselves as children and were acting out.... But millions of women are raped, and they do not rape anyone in return. Simple cause-and-effect victimization theories are just that—simple. Something much larger than individual pathology is involved. Rape is a hate crime, the logical outcome of an ancient social bias against women. We must not forget that it is supported by a system of language, law, and custom.[32]

Working with individual pathology is not enough. With each of our steps toward building nonviolent communities we must remember the social context from which violence is created and address also all other inequalities, including those places of sexism, heterosexism, racism and classism in each of us. Raising public awareness of both the causes and costs of violence requires work in both private and public sectors—with parents, children, teachers, clergy, judges, police and legislators. Caring support systems for those wanting to end the violence in their lives are often underfunded and co-opted from community-defined and directed services to private or institutionally controlled programs; this too must be addressed.

WE CANNOT BE EQUAL UNTIL WE CAN BE DIFFERENT IN OUR OWN WAYS, NOT THOSE IMPOSED ON US.
—*Elizabeth K. Minnid*

Recovery of our basic humanity needs to occur in as many ways as possible. We don't need a whole industry of social services to create changes in our own lives, although necessary and diverse resources for recovery are essential and desperately lacking for funds. We do need social sanctioning of improved living conditions for women and children—observable, concrete, material conditions that enable women to be self-determining, healthy, economically independent, and safe. We can begin with the resources closest to us: our openness to learn and dream about living without violence, our willingness to speak clearly to injustices, and our commitment to creative social change work that ensures the material conditions necessary to keep women from sliding into homelessness and poverty.

TAXATION AND LABOR LAWS, ECONOMIC, INCOME AND WELFARE REGULATIONS: THEY CAN PRODUCE MORE FAMILY PATHOLOGIES THAN ANY FAMILY SERVICE CAN CURE.
—*Family Violence in a Patriarchal Culture Manual*

6. From cynicism to collaboration

All violence is the result of great alienation from the fragility and preciousness of all our lives. Life, this great gift, is forgotten in a plethora of greed, individualism and fear. Violent behavior often is the will to dominate and the obsession for more—compulsions that have taken greed and exploitation nearly as far as they can go. Competition and greed, if continued at the present pace, threatens 500,000 species of plants and animals by the year 2000.[33] Whole races of people have been exterminated in the name of commerce and nationalism. The belief in this right has despiritualized and dehumanized our lives.

Details of abuse are shocking but listening to survivors of assault gives us the information we need to know in order to effect change. Despair and disbelief are common emotional responses to hearing such stories, but they can be transformed into powerful action if we take time to fully listen to one another and draw support from the potential that exists between us. Cynicism and negativism are easy to find and stand as important clues that the world is in need of profound care and deep healing. This can begin by acknowledging that the interdependence of all life has become a fragile web weakened by the politics of profit and militarism.

It is a great challenge to disarm psychological and physical defences, but it is the only way forward. Anger, when directed without harm, can mobilize great change. But the relief and joy that result from building nonviolence in our lives and communities can be the most motivating force behind constructive, lasting change. Can we find ways to reconcile with victims and perpetrators? Are we willing to address the underlying issues of power, sexuality and spirituality that violence against women has exposed? We can refuse to further the international and intergenerational legacy of violence by developing collaborative practices based on nonviolent resistance, healing and generosity.

WHAT IS WAR?
WAR IS TAKING
WHAT HAS NOT
BEEN OFFERED.
WHAT IS THE
OPPOSITE OF WAR?
GIFTS.
    —DEENA METZGER

Notes

[1] *Women in The Front Line: Human Rights Violations Against Women— An Amnesty International Report* (New York: Amnesty International Publications, 1990).

[2] See Catharine MacKinnon, "Turning Rape into Pornography: Postmodern Genocide," *Ms.*, July/August, 1993, pp. 24-30; Laureen Pitter and Alexander Stitglmayer, "Will the World Remember? Will the World Forget?," *Ms.*, April/May, 1993, pp. 12-13, 19-22.

[3] Catharine MacKinnon, "Turning Rape into Pornography," p. 27.

[4] Ibid., p. 28.

[5] Ron Thorne-Finch, *Ending the Silence: The Origins and Treatment of*

Male Violence against Women (Toronto: University of Toronto Press, 1992), p. 89.

[6] In *Stopping Rape: A Challenge for Men* (Philadelphia & Gabriola Island: New Society Publishers, 1993), p. 52.

[7] Ibid., p. 50.

[8] In *Transforming A Rape Culture*, ed. Buchwald, Fletcher and Roth (Minneapolis: Milkweed Edition, 1994) p. 389.

[9] *Right Wing Women* (New York: Perigee Books, 1982), p. 197.

[10] Steven Hill and Nina Silver, "Antipornography Legislation: Addressing the Harm to Women," in *Transforming a Rape Culture*, ed. Buchwald, Fletcher and Roth (Minneapolis: Milkweed Editions, 1994), p. 289.

[11] See the work of John Briere, Susan Brownmiller, Edward Donnerstein, Susan Gubar, Joan Hoff, Neil Malamuth, Susan Mayerson, Steven Penrod, Diana Russell, Dalma Taylor and others for studies on pornography, aggression and sexual assault. See Ron Thorne-Finch for overview.

[12] Quoted in Thorne-Finch, *Ending the Silence*, p. 91. *Not a Love Story* was written and produced by Bonnie Klein, National Film Board, 1981.

[13] Gloria Steinem, "Erotica vs. Pornography," in *Transforming a Rape Culture*, p. 36.

[14] Hill and Silver, "Civil Rights Antipornography Legislation: Addressing the Harm to Women," in *Transforming a Rape Culture*, pp. 283-299.

[15] See Anne Jones, *Next Time, She'll Be Dead: Battering and How to Stop It* (Boston: Beacon Press, 1994), p. 116 and Diana E. H. Russell, *Rape in Marriage* (1982), pp. 83-86.

[16] Anne Jones, *Next Time, She'll Be Dead*, p. 117.

[17] Statistics Canada: *The Violence Against Women Survey, Highlights*, Ottawa: Minister Responsible for Statistics Canada, November 1993.

Stopping the Violence: A Safer Future for BC Women, Fact Sheet No. 2, the statistics: Violence Against Women in Canada, Victoria: Ministry of Women's Equality, 1993.

Statistics Canada: *Wife Assault: The Findings of the National Survey*, Karen Rodgers, Ottawa, Canadian Centre for Justice Statistics, Vol. 4, #9, 1994.

Statistics Canada, *Spousal Homicide*, Margo Wilson and Martin Daly, Department of Psychology, McMaster University, Ottawa,

Canadian Centre for Justice Statistics, Minister Responsible for Statistics, Vol. 14, #9, 1994.

[18] Ibid.

[19] Haki R. Madhubuti, "On Becoming Anti-Rapist," in *Transforming a Rape Culture*, p. 167.

[20] "No More! Stopping Domestic Violence," *Ms.* V, #2 (Sept./Oct. 1994): 42.

[21] Evan Stark and Anne Flitcraft, "Women and Children at Risk: A Feminist Perspective on Child Abuse," *International Journal of Health Services* 18, #1 (1988); Linda McKibben et al., "Victimization of Mothers of Abused Children: A Controlled Study," *Pediatrics* 84, #3 (1989). These references are noted by Anne Jones in *Next Time, She'll Be Dead*, p. 85.

[22] Christine Wright and Jean Pierre Leroux, "Children As Victims of Violent Crime, Ottawa: Statistics Canada 11, #8, 1991.

[23] Linda Macleod, *Battered But Not Beaten* (Ottawa: Canadian Advisory Council on the Status of Women, 1987).

[24] Robin Morgan, *The Demon Lover: On the Sexuality of Terrorism* (New York: W.W. Norton & Company, 1989), p. 334.

[25] See Lenore Walker, Linda Macleod.

[26] Anne Jones, *Next Time She'll Be Dead: Battering and How to Stop It* (Boston: Beacon Press, 1994), p. 87.

[27] Quotes are taken from a letter from Judy Webb, August 26, 1994. With permission.

[28] Amnesty International, *Report on Torture*, 1973.

[29] "I Just Raped My Wife! What Are You Going to Do About It Pastor?: The Church and Sexual Violence," in *Transforming a Rape Culture*, p. 74.

[30] In *Transforming a Rape Culture*, p. 167.

[31] Ibid.

[32] Ibid., pp. 51-52.

[33] Margo Adair, *Working Inside Out: Tools for Change* (Berkeley: Wingbow Press, 1984).

II FEMINISM AND NONVIOLENCE

1. You can't kill the spirit

Feminism is a way of seeing the world. The description, analysis, vision and strategy of feminism may change according to one's race, nationality or class.[1] But common to all forms of feminism is an analysis of authoritarian systems and patriarchal doctrines of domination, exploitation and subordination; doctrines based on a presumed male "right to conquest" through unrelenting forms of destruction and terrorism. The colonization of tribal bodies, women's bodies, Earth's bodies, and the devastation of the spirit in all living forms, has only through a feminist analysis come anywhere near to being coherently addressed. Feminists for centuries have committed their life's work to bearing witness and bringing understanding to the horrors all around us. In the midst of countless deaths, diaspora and displacements, feminism has opened a world mostly closed to women and others who have been pushed to the margins.

Feminism has given voice to women where before there was little, and with this voice comes a rejection of "oppressive regimes of being" and "oligarchies of the spirit."[2] Feminism imagines a world without rape, an absence of misogyny and all other forms of violence based on a logic of racial or sexual superiority. It supports the development of ideas and alternatives that respect the diversity and commonality of humankind. If offers a model of democracy based on participatory rather than leader-based strength, and uses of power that cherish rather than destroy life.

Ultimately, feminism supports the liberation of individuals and whole nations of people from oppression. Critical to the vision of liberation is an examination of the use of global resources and the restoration of their equitable redistribution. As Charlotte Bunch wrote in 1985, "A feminist vision must address what kind of living and what forms of distributing resources would improve the quality of life for all people while preserving the world's resources for the

IT IS QUITE STRANGE...THAT AS YET THERE IS NO SUCH THING AS A SCIENCE OF PEACE, SINCE THE SCIENCE OF WAR APPEARS TO BE HIGHLY ADVANCED, AT LEAST REGARDING SUCH CONCRETE SUBJECTS AS ARMAMENTS AND STRATEGY. AS A COLLECTIVE HUMAN PHENOMENON, HOWEVER, EVEN WAR INVOLVES MYSTERY, FOR ALL THE PEOPLE OF THE EARTH, WHO PROFESS TO BE EAGER TO BANISH WAR AS THE WORST OF SCOURGES, ARE NONETHELESS THE VERY ONES WHO CONCUR IN THE STARTING OF WARS AND WHO WILLINGLY SUPPORT ARMED COMBAT.
—*Maria Montessori*

27

survival of future generations."[3]

Feminism has been and will continue to be suspicious of the extreme power of large corporations to oppress, and so it advocates forms of democracy that are decentralized, citizen-centred and protective of the human spirit.

Just as a tradition of feminism reaches for more than the absence of sexism, the tradition of nonviolence strives for more than the absence of violence. While feminism works for freedom from constraint, nonviolence reaches for lasting liberation. Combined, the two traditions form a rich dialectic of insight and action. The early days of feminism, which articulated "the personal is political," have deepened into a far-reaching exploration of the intimate connection between internal and external freedom.

As we will consider in Chapter 3, this requires understanding the forms of power available to us and choosing to use power in ways that are beneficial to all. Joanne Sheehan in her paper "Nonviolence: A Feminist Vision and Strategy," defines nonviolence as

> acting on the belief that we have the power to resist power-over-us through noncompliance, exercising the power-to-be who we choose to be. We refuse to be victims, to violate our own conscience. We refuse to be passive, to ignore justice.[4]

Here, the self-determination of feminism calls for a strength of resistance and restoration of the right to exist without violence. In the same article, Helen Michalowski writes how

> power from a nonviolent perspective is expressed in terms of empowerment of ourselves and of others sharing, communicating, creating an alternative social order which draws boundless strength from having incorporated the differences of everyone's reality.[5]

This collaboration of nonviolence and feminism invites both men and women to examine how dominant structures have an impact on our lives, to resist demoralization and dehumanization, and to build a new politic based on the transformation possible when feminism and nonviolence combine in efforts of resistance and recovery.

2. Freedom struggles

The use of nonviolence is as old or older than recorded history.

There have been numerous instances of people who have courageously and nonviolently refused complicity with injustice. In *You Can't Kill the Spirit* and *This River of Courage*, Pam McAllister chronicles hundreds of examples of nonviolent action used by women around the world in struggles for social justice.[6] What is relatively new however, in the history of nonviolent action, is the fusion of nonviolent action with mass struggle. Organized warfare is at least 30 centuries old, but organized nonviolent action as we know it is less than one century old.

The synthesis of mass struggle and nonviolence was developed in the freedom struggle of India and pioneered by Mahatma Gandhi, who led a nation to independence through a spiritual activism of nonviolence. In Japan, since the atomic bombing of Hiroshima and Nagasaki, many Japanese Buddhists have been tireless witnesses against war. Throughout Latin America, Servico Paz y Justico is working for a liberation that includes both justice and peace. The Mothers of Plaza de Mayo in Argentina are a group of women who demonstrated peacefully over the years to show the government that their "disappeared" children and husbands had not been forgotten. The brutal Marcos dictatorship in the Philippines was overthrown by masses of unarmed people who simply refused to co-operate and poured out into the streets in an unprecedented "people power" revolution. In 1989 and 1990 totalitarian governments in Eastern Europe collapsed not from military attack but from the unarmed resistance of the people.

Nonviolent demonstrations for women's suffrage led to the passage of a Constitutional amendment guaranteeing women the right to vote. The U.S. civil rights movement won passage of the Civil Rights Act of 1964 and the Voting Rights Act of 1965 through dauntless nonviolent activism. The anti-slavery and labor movements are historically rich with examples of successful nonviolent action. And the battered women's movement, an internationally strong alliance, is ongoing in its activism for release from domestic violence, examples of which will be illustrated in Chapter 9. The list goes on.[7]

...IF YOU INSIST UPON FIGHTING TO PROTECT ME, OR "OUR" COUNTRY, LET IT BE UNDERSTOOD, SOBERLY AND RATIONALLY BETWEEN US, THAT YOU ARE FIGHTING TO GRATIFY A SEX INSTINCT WHICH I CANNOT SHARE; BUT NOT TO GRATIFY MY INSTINCTS, OR TO PROTECT EITHER MYSELF OR MY COUNTRY. FOR, THE OUTSIDER WILL SAY, IN FACT, AS A WOMAN, I HAVE NO COUNTRY. AS A WOMAN I WANT NO MORE COUNTRY. AS A WOMAN MY COUNTRY IS THE WHOLE WORLD....
—*VIRGINIA WOOLF*

3. Change, not vengeance

We can respond to violence in many ways. Acting nonviolently means we do not seek revenge or retaliation for injustice done to ourselves and others. Barbara Deming's decades of work investigating the relationship of feminism to strategical nonviolence made clear her belief that what is essential to human liberation is not revenge but respect for fundamental rights. *Vengeance*, she wrote, *was not the point. Change is.* By joining feminism and nonviolence, there is a healing beyond resistance that includes the essential realization of our interconnectedness, coexistence and mutuality. Emphasizing our interconnections brings hope to our children. Proving the possibilities of change through nonviolent activism, we show our children the way to peace. Instilling the presence of justice for abuses creates the retribution necessary to move onward to living without violence.

AS MY SUFFERING MOUNTED I SOON REALIZED THAT THERE WERE TWO WAYS I COULD RESPOND TO MY SITUATION—EITHER TO REACT WITH BITTERNESS OR SEEK TO TRANSFORM THE SUFFERING INTO A CREATIVE FORCE.
—*MARTIN LUTHER KING JR.*

Fundamental to any concept of social justice is the belief that without respect for basic human rights, peace cannot be restored in our families, communities and nations. Holding ourselves accountable is a commitment that can range from simple to complicated acts of courage. Feminism has awakened critical consciousness; by linking the oppressive larger political systems governing most of the world with oppressive systems dominating most families, we can see where to begin with ourselves.

Wherever and however we are living we are all called to look at our own lives with an openness to nonviolent change. We can work with ourselves, our families and the systems binding our lives together. We can look at the personal and political meaning of how we live our lives.

4. A life-saving balance

Nonviolence springs from the uniqueness of spirit and deliberate intention in each of us to create models of loving that affirm the dignity of all citizens. To develop healing models that are inclusive, we depend on the individual and local creativity of each of our communities. Our first service in a community is to help each other heal our injuries and fears, carefully converting the seeds of divisions we carry within to an acceptance that each of us belongs in our communities.

IT'S A POLITIC OF AFFINITY. WE DON'T TRY TO DENY OR MANIPULATE INDIVIDUAL DIFFERENCE.
—*RAM DASS*

We can find ways to affirm what is truly valuable in each of our community members and look for ways to resist and eventually transform the oppression in our lives. As Deming explains:

> In nonviolent struggle, we seek to hold in mind both contradiction and commonality. We refuse to co-operate with that which is in

contradiction to our deep needs; and we speak to that commonality linking us all which, if remembered, can inhibit the impulse to destroy. A nonviolent dialectic—that is the dialectic that I do think accords with feminism and that we must try to invent.[8]

This is using the two hands of nonviolence (See Chapter 3, section 4). It underlies feminist sensibility in refusing to be victims and refusing to be violent, whenever possible. The oppressed in the oppressor is not ignored. In this approach there is no *other*; there is no enemy. Some argue this is passive; however, in Deming's words, "it can be a much more passive, much more desperate act to reply in kind—to accept as one's own the oppressor's vision that there is nothing at all to prevent us from trying to destroy one another."[9]

The partnership of feminist self-assertion and nonviolent mutual respect is a life-saving balance that gives us strength to challenge that which cripples our humanity and to restore that which builds community. *This life-saving balance—this equilibrium between self-assertion and respect for others—has evolved among animals on a physiological plane. In human beings it can be gained only on the plane of consciousness. One can, it seems, only love another as one loves oneself.*[10] We are looking for a politic rooted in the spirit of love—one seemingly extinct but one we can revitalize in our refusal to be victims or violators.

5. Reclaiming our bodies

Feminists are bringing forward another vision, a different kind of intelligence that leaves behind the unreasonableness of terror and violence and searches for something with reason. We turn away from a consciousness that feeds terror and disconnection from one another and allow ourselves to dream, to love joyfully and humanely, and to act boldly by breaking our silence with a voice different from *the old story of death* and degradation. There is an incredible movement toward a wholeness that is imagined and activated by a *simple desire for life*. We are learning with many other women and men that "only a deep attention to the whole of our life can bring us the capacity to love well and freely."[11]

We embrace the instincts of our bodies and begin celebrating the unpredictable nature of the multiple and variant patterns that affirm this energy. As unharmed children know, our freedom comes

I THINK THE ONLY CHOICE THAT WILL ENABLE US TO HOLD TO OUR VISION WITHOUT BEING SCARED INTO WANTING TO RETREAT [FROM FEMINISM] IS ONE THAT...ADOPTS A CONCEPT FAMILIAR TO THE NONVIOLENT TRADITION: NAMING BEHAVIOR THAT IS OPPRESSIVE, NAMING ABUSE OF POWER THAT IS HELD UNFAIRLY AND MUST BE DESTROYED, BUT NAMING NO ONE PERSON WHOM WE ARE WILLING TO DESTROY.
—*Barbara Deming*

SEXUAL INTELLIGENCE WOULD HAVE TO BE ROOTED FIRST AND FOREMOST IN THE HONEST POSSESSION OF ONE'S OWN BODY.
—*Andrea Dworkin*

from trusting in our own knowledge, living fully in our bodies and self-determining a love that denies not one spark of creative life. We repossess our bodies and our minds and through this empowerment recover our souls. In this we find self-respect, an excitement for living, a mindfulness in movement, and a real sense of belonging.

I WOULD BELIEVE
MY PAIN.
—THEODORE ROETKE

Our only choice is to begin by turning first to ourselves and healing our brokenness—the places we have been split in two, severed and silenced. Regaining control over our bodies is a necessary homecoming awaiting us all. In a world where we cannot control the violence, Pamela Fletcher enjoins us,

> ...we must take control over our bodies. In protecting ourselves, we must realize that we cannot continue to disassociate our bodies from our souls. We must claim ourselves as whole human beings. When we are empowered physically, we are both spiritually and physically strong. Being in tune with our bodies helps us to trust our instincts.[12]

6. Trusting our instincts

Clarissa Pinkola Estés writes:

> All women must acknowledge that both within and without, there is a force which will act in opposition to the instincts of the natural Self, and that that malignant force *is what it is*. Though we might have mercy upon it, our first actions must be to recognize it, to protect ourselves from its devastations, and ultimately to deprive it of its murderous energy.
>
> All creatures must learn that there exist predators. Without this knowing, a woman will be unable to negotiate safely within her own forest without being devoured. To understand the predator is to become a mature animal who is not vulnerable out of naiveté, inexperience, or foolishness.[13]

I TAKE UP AGAIN
EACH MORNING
THE LABOR OF
LEARNING TO
KNOW WHAT IT
IS THAT I REALLY
DO KNOW.
—BARBARA DEMING

We need to protect ourselves from the devastation of the predator—that which preys on women and children's lives and is compelled to kill the instinctive or the natural self. This is how we empower ourselves to act, and from this, establish personal action that becomes local and eventually, global in meaning and effect.

This is not easy in a society where most women are prevented from determining their own lives and where most children are taught to disassociate at an early age from the instinctive, the mysterious and the awesome beauty of the natural world. We need to turn away from attitudes and behaviors that shame the body and induce the belief that children and women are not entitled to themselves. We can encourage ways of living that deepen self-governance with balance, care and self-worth. Out of this is born a reciprocity and respect that knows no form of exploitation or degradation.

In West Africa there is a belief that to be harsh with a child is to cause its soul to retreat from its body. Liberating our bodies from images and actions bent on destroying the soul means determining for ourselves a definition of life free from internalized misogyny and inferiority. "When our souls are connected to our bodies," Pamela Fletcher tells us, "we do not allow our bodies to be taken for granted or to be taken away from us—at least not without a struggle."[14] An instinctual way of living does not reject the body we are born with. Instead, it learns to honor its uniqueness, its stories and capabilities. It allows us to be self-represented and self-realized. Our instincts often tell us when touch is not welcomed or wanted, and when it is. We know too that the body of another must be respected—that if we are destructive in our thinking about who we are we will be destructive in our relations with others.

> HERE IN THIS BODY ARE THE SACRED RIVERS: HERE ARE THE SUN AND MOON, AS WELL AS PILGRIMAGE PLACES. I HAVE NOT ENCOUNTERED ANOTHER TEMPLE AS BLISSFUL AS MY BODY.
>
> —SARAHA

Feminism has moved us closer to taking up the responsibility of healing the many fractures our bodysoul suffers. We owe this to ourselves so a practice of joy in our wholeness is embodied and exclaimed with great fierceness. We can learn to lean toward a living that nurtures our wholeness. If we do not know this in ourselves we need to look for those in our communities who do embody this knowledge—whose wholeness resounds with self-acceptance, compassion and courage. Let's find the friends and advocates in our communities who are "prepared to demonstrate that strength has many ways of being expressed and coercion has no place in intimate relations, not to mention its diminishing value in our global community."[15] Let's bear witness to this kind of courage and strength in women and men whenever we can and allow our children to learn this freely and independently.

> I WOULD HOPE THAT EVEN IN THE MOST EXTREME EXILE THERE WOULD BE A FORCE GREATER THAN EVERYTHING, A FORCE WHICH CONTINUES TO SING: WHAT CELAN CALLS THE SINGHARREST—THE SINGABLE REMAINS.
>
> —HÉLÈNE CIXOUS

So many are saying the climate is right for this change to happen. We have not been taught well how to be men and women but the opportunities being offered to us to take part in a conspiracy of nonviolent collaboration and deep healing are all around. We need only look beyond the patriarchal lens and see a whole new vista waiting.

Notes

[1] See Joanne Sheehan, "Nonviolence: A Feminist Vision and Strategy," from *Daring to Change: Perspectives on Feminism and Nonviolence* (War Resisters League: New York), p. 3. This is the framework laid out by Charlotte Bunch, 1983, "Not be Degrees: Feminist Theory and Education," in *Learning Our Way: Essays in Feminist Education*, eds., Charlotte Bunch and Sandra Pollack (Trumansburg, N.Y.: The Crossing Press), pp. 248-60.

[2] Inés Hernadez-Avila, "In Praise of Insubordination, or What Makes a Good Woman Go Bad?," in *Transforming a Rape Culture*, ed. Buchwald, Fletcher and Roth (Minneapolis: Milkweed Editions, 1994), p. 378.

[3] Charlotte Bunch, *Going Public with Our Vision* (Denver: Antelope Publications, 1985).

[4] Quoted in Sheehan, "Nonviolence: A Feminist Vision and Strategy," p. 3.

[5] Ibid.

[6] These books are invaluable sources of inspiration and education. Pam McAllister documents with clarity and detail what has long been missing from traditional history texts.

[7] For reference see "Historical Examples of Nonviolent Struggle" (Cambridge, Ma.: Albert Einstein Institute); Ed Hedemann, "Nonviolence"; *Handbook for Nonviolent Action* (NY: War Resisters League, 1991); and Pam McAllister, *You Can't Kill the Spirit* (Philadelphia & Gabriola Island: New Society Publishers, 1989) and *This River of Courage* (1991).

[8] Jane Meyerding, ed., *We Are All Part of One Another: A Barbara Deming Reader* (Philadelphia & Gabriola Island: New Society Publishers, 1984), p. 290.

[9] Ibid., p. 289.

[10] Ibid., p. 188.

[11] Jack Kornfield, *A Path of the Heart* (New York: Bantam Books, 1994), p. 249.

[12] Pamela R. Fletcher, "Whose Body Is It, Anyway? Transforming Ourselves to Change a Rape Culture" in *Transforming a Rape Culture*, ed. Buchwald, Fletcher and Roth (Minneapolis: Milkweed Editions, 1994), p. 439.

[13] Clarissa Pinkola Estés, *Women Who Run With the Wolves* (New York: Ballantine Books, 1992), p. 46.

[14] *Transforming a Rape Culture*, p. 438.

[15] W.J. Musa Moore-Foster, "Up From Brutality" in *Transforming a Rape Culture*, p. 424.

III   PRINCIPLES AND PRACTICES OF NONVIOLENCE

1. Resisting amnesia

The principles and practices of many nonviolence traditions demonstrate a way of living that honors all life. An ecology of living is sought that brings balance, dignity and health to livelihood and loving. This involves deep listening to what is going on in the world and an active search for freedom from violence. Nonviolence practices, when extended from the self to others, effect social change, often through justice work. Nonviolent work for justice resists amnesia (the habit of forgetting historical process and responsibility) by insisting on accountability and care. We ask ourselves and others to wake up and to be conscious of the inner and external forces shaping our lives.

THE FIRST THING TO BE DISRUPTED BY OUR COMMITMENT TO NONVIOLENCE WILL NOT BE THE SYSTEM BUT OUR OWN LIVES.
—JIM DOUGLASS

Nonviolence requires imagination—the capacity to open to possibilities of living without oppression. It also requires courage—the willingness to witness our lives and those around us with truth and with as much accuracy as possible: what Quakers describe as speaking truth to power. This is the recognition of the history of social inequality and the scrupulous examination of legacies of oppression passed on generation to generation. When strategically turned toward injustice, nonviolence is a dynamic movement of ending discrimination and persecution and taking responsibility for the history created in our lives now. It is the effort to understand one's own history and the connectedness (or disconnectedness) of our lives with others. In her essay "Resisting Amnesia," Adrienne Rich explains:

WHILE SILENCE IS THE OPPOSITE OF SPEAKING, DENIAL IS THE OPPOSITE OF NAMING.
—CAROL J. ADAMS

> Historical amnesia *is* starvation of the imagination; nostalgia is the imagination's sugar rush, leaving depression and emptiness in its wake. Breaking silences, telling our tales, is not enough. We can value that process—and the courage it may require—without believing that it is an end in itself. Historical responsibility has, after all, to do with action—where we place the weight of our

existences on the line, cast our lot with others, move from an individual consciousness to a collective one: How did we come to be where we are and not elsewhere?[1]

Nostalgia deceives the past by grasping only what wants to be remembered and wiping out whole realities. Can we look carefully at what and how humanity has been lost as well as gained, without erasing the lives of others from our memories and stories? Can we move toward an *embodied* account of history, one that is full of both the seen and not seen contexts of our lives? Can Western civilization move from its uncivilized centre of control and learn to unoccupy that space? The nostalgia of oppressors is very select; it is a refusal of the full story, or standing somewhere else and allowing others to speak.

Resisting amnesia is refusing to lie. "White men," Rich writes, "need a history that does not simply 'include' peoples of color and white women, but that shows the process by which the arrogance of hierarchy and the celebration of violence have reached a point of destructiveness almost out of control. In other words, white men need to start questioning the text handed down from father to son, the dominator's version."[2] Nonviolence justice work looks to remedy what is displaced and repossess what is missing.

What do we want to conserve and continue in the living texts handed down father to son, mother to daughter, from one gender to the other, from the nation-state to its populace? What do we want to ensure we do not repeat? Will the genocide of indigenous people; the rape of women and children; the racial discrimination of Asians, Latin Americans, blacks; the dispossession of immigrants; the gas-lighting of gays and lesbians continue to be tolerated another decade, another century?

The principles behind the traditions of nonviolence serve to activate the accountable and just use of power in all relationships. This power serves the imaginative remapping of life without violence, the creation of texts of love that reform relationship to a place of real dignity and not the false autocracy of arrogance or entitlement, and the recovery and rewriting of history—or herstory—that has been denied. The practice of nonviolence is a resistance to assimilation—refusing to become who we are not, to appropriate what does not belong to us, to abandon our histories, and to accept the history texts that celebrate violence. Nonviolence, then, becomes a practice of self-definition in alliance with others

HISTORY IS THE
VERSION OF EVENTS
TOLD BY
CONQUERORS,
THE DOMINATORS.
—ADRIENNE RICH

IF YOU DO NOT
TELL THE TRUTH
ABOUT YOURSELF
YOU CANNOT
TELL IT ABOUT
OTHER PEOPLE.
—VIRGINIA WOOLF

who also seek a non-injurious and mutually strengthening assertion of life.

2. Healing the inner war

Collectively, an oppressed people may look back on their history and recognize that there was not only oppression but self- injury....[3] There are the self-destructive acts we perpetrate on our own lives by abandoning the reality, feelings and gifts of our own lives—by pretending to live another life, by pushing away yearnings for imaginative expression, by undermining choice, and by disassociating from the natural world.

Disassociation in many forms runs deep in North American society. It is the by-product of self-hatred and survival mechanisms that obliterate our true selves, and that we have been taught and continue to teach ourselves. It is crucial, as we reach for nonviolence in our lives, that we not delete aspects of ourselves from our memory. In many ways, nonviolence traditions are attempts to come home to lives free from deceit and dehumanization. They are a way of drawing strength from self-knowledge and learning to use that strength for collective purposes.

Active nonviolence requires thinking with the heart, and living with awareness. This is a practice of mindfulness in all our relationships, beginning with our own selves. A nonviolent self requires we deeply connect and listen to our own lives, that we care for our inner life with courage to face whatever is there. It is turning with love to the places we fear in our own nature and bringing careful attention to see what is needed.

In each of our lives are places of pain and fear. Unattended, our wounds and confusions grow into numbness and conflict. Inner conflict will eventually affect all our relationships. In Buddhist practice, it is said to be necessary "to take the one seat" in order to bring the presence of mind and heart that is needed to live mindfully. Taking the one seat is choosing to be present with whatever is there, a presence that does not reject what it finds but seeks to understand and heal. As Jack Kornfield teaches:

THE TRUE FOCUS OF REVOLUTIONARY CHANGE IS NEVER MERELY THE OPPRESSIVE SITUATIONS WHICH WE SEEK TO ESCAPE, BUT THAT PIECE OF THE OPPRESSOR WHICH IS PLANTED DEEP WITHIN EACH OF US, AND WHICH KNOWS ONLY THE OPPRESSORS' TACTICS, THE OPPRESSORS' RELATIONSHIPS.

—Audre Lorde

> Stopping the war and becoming present are two sides of the same activity. To come into the present is to stop the war. To come into the present means to experience what is here and now. Most of us have spent our lives caught up in plans, expectations, ambitions for the future, in regrets, guilt or shame about the past.

When we come into the present, we begin to feel the life around us again, but we also encounter what we have been avoiding. We must have the courage to face whatever is present—our pain, our desires, our grief, our loss, our secret hopes, our love—everything that moves us deeply. As we stop the war, each of us will find something from which we have been running—our loneliness, our unworthiness, our boredom, our shame, our unfulfilled desires. We must face these parts of ourselves as well.[4]

If we cannot find ways of taking the one seat, the inner war will continue. Avoidance of pain and fear is manifested through denial, then addictions, alienation, depression and violence. We become merciless with what is crying most for mercy. The effort to bring mercy to the enemies within is essential if our effort to stop the outer wars is to succeed.

Transformation doesn't happen overnight or by accident. It begins with ourselves and a willingness to risk loving those aspects of ourselves that are most tormented. None of us is exempt from the sorrows and suffering encountered in this world. We need to commit ourselves in an ongoing way in order to be present with where we are most divided.

3. Satyagraha

Mohandas Karamchand Gandhi (1869-1948) taught the principles of nonviolence as *satyagraha*. *Satya* implies truth and *graha*, firmness, thus the meaning is to live by firmly grasping one's truth, often translated as truth-force. *Satyagraha* is the path of *ahimsa* or non-harming action based on truth of being through *active love*. This is a form of loving that rests in a strength of self based on honest and inward looking, and clear and assertive action. Many traditions of nonviolence teach that only through active love can the practice of enemy thinking be conquered. It is love based on insight, constancy and courage. *In satyagraha*, Gandhi taught, *the cause has to be just and clear as well as the means.*[5]

In an overview of Gandhi and the imperative of nonviolence, Charlene Spretnak explains that *Gandhi was convinced that the power of love is the same as the power of truth, a force without which the universe would disappear.* Gandhi taught:

> The law of love will work, just as the law of gravitation will work, whether we accept it or not.... The more I work at this law the more I feel delight in life, the delight in the scheme of this universe. It gives me peace and a meaning of the mysteries of the nature that I have no power to describe.[6]

ALTHOUGH AT
TIMES THE MIND
MAY NOT BE CLEAR,
COMPASSION
IS ALWAYS
THE APPROPRIATE
RESPONSE. TO HAVE
MERCY ON OUR
MERCILESSNESS. TO
LEAVE NOTHING
UNHEALED.
—STEPHEN LEVINE

LOVE IS THE
SEQUENCE OF
LONG DAYS/
AT SEA,
WITHOUT RELIEF,/
AND LOVE
IS THE IMPROBABLE/
RETURN OF
THE DOVE/
CARRYING IN
ITS BEAK/
THE GREEN LEAF.
—BARBARA DEMING

Transformation of violence depends on the firmness of nonviolent intention behind social action. *Satyagraha* shapes the way we view each other and respond to our conditions. It is an endless effort in which spiritual discipline informs social action. The principles of nonviolence ground the spirit within the practices of political action. A satyagrahi is "totally devoted to the transformation of his own life, of his adversary, and of society by means of love."[7] This is a devotion that looks at violence and its face of terror without wanting to hurt back and instead, moves toward any opening that acts in accord with peace. Thomas Merton explained it this way:

> Since *himsa* (violence) degrades and corrupts man, to meet force with force and hatred with hatred only increases man's progressive degeneration. Nonviolence, on the contrary, heals and restores man's nature, while giving him a means to restore social order and justice. *Ahimsa* is not a policy for the seizure of power. It is a way of transforming relationships so as to bring about a peaceful transfer of power, effected freely and without compulsion by all concerned, because all have to recognize it as right.[8]

CHRIST KNEW ALSO, JUST AS ALL REASONABLE HUMAN BEINGS MUST KNOW, THAT THE EMPLOYMENT OF VIOLENCE IS INCOMPATIBLE WITH LOVE, WHICH IS THE FUNDAMENTAL LAW OF LIFE.
—LEO TOLSTOY

4. Two-handed approach

We need alternatives to violence when we experience hurt and defensiveness. As Martin Luther King said, *The eye-for-an-eye philosophy leaves everybody blind.* At no other time in history has nonviolence been more needed. The choice we have now, which King and other social spiritual activists expostulated, is not between nonviolence and violence but rather between nonviolence and non-existence.

A principle of nonviolent action is that of non-co-operation with everything humiliating. This includes non-co-operation with dehumanizing images of each other that deny the possibility of transformation. We can recognize how we make enemies by naming someone an enemy. By refusing to view all sides of our experiences we live only half-heartedly. Our responses need to support insight gained by both sides. This way there is benefit for all and we avoid the deficit of winners and losers. The work of nonviolence depends on a resistance that is open to change and is "two-handed." Here, nonviolence means refusing to be a victim while reaching out to the suffering in the abuser. We can simultaneously reject

AS YOU PRESS ON FOR JUSTICE, BE SURE TO MOVE WITH DIGNITY AND DISCIPLINE, USING ONLY THE WEAPONS OF LOVE.
—MARTIN LUTHER KING JR.

dehumanizing behavior while respecting the dignity due all.

This has traditionally been defined as the two-handed approach and can create a "moral ju-jitsu"[9] in which the offender is decentred by the victim,

> combining nonviolent discipline with solidarity and persistence in struggle. The nonviolent actionists cause the violence of the opponent's repression to be exposed.... This, in turn, may lead to shifts in opinion and then to shifts in power relationships....[10]

Here, the attacker loses moral balance. Ju-Jitsu is a Japanese system of unarmed combat using an opponent's strength and weight to his disadvantage. Used in a context of contemporary nonviolent resistance, the offender is decentered by the victim's strength of nonviolent skill. By using skill, not force, the nonviolent practitioner lets the attacker be defeated by his own momentum.[11] This form of action looks for the human face behind the enemy image and in this, a possible transformation of relationship.

5. Self-governance

The way to peace in families and communities is to govern ourselves lovingly. Nonviolence does not seek revenge or retaliation for injustice done to ourselves and others. The goal is change—the transformation of self and other—while seeking truth and justice for all. This transformation requires self-respect or ways of governing ourselves without harm. It is a form of power that resides within ourselves and draws its strength from respecting the dignity and worthiness of all human beings.

Power that increases self-respect does not depend on external authority. It is increased through awareness of self in relationship and by making choices about how to exercise that awareness. The intentions governing our inner will are not separate from our outer actions. If the inner law is nonviolence, then external law will be affected.

Can we choose to see the immense power that resides in each of us for communitarian benefit and govern ourselves accordingly? During a discussion with Judith Plant, Marie Wilson explains that in the Gitskan language there is no word for "rights." The closest they come to any equivalent, we are told, is "jurisdiction and responsibility." The responsibilities are the ways a person chooses to govern him or herself with all beings. Right relationship for the

NONVIOLENCE MEANS AVOIDING NOT ONLY EXTERNAL PHYSICAL VIOLENCE BUT ALSO INTERNAL VIOLENCE OF SPIRIT. YOU NOT ONLY REFUSE TO SHOOT A MAN, BUT YOU REFUSE TO HATE HIM.

—MARTIN LUTHER KING JR.

THE EXPERIENCE OF INTERCONNECTION WITH ALL LIFE CAN SUSTAIN OUR SOCIAL CHANGE WORK FAR BETTER THAN RIGHTEOUS PARTISANSHIP.

—JOANNA MACY

Gitskan lies between self-authority and responsibility to others.[12]

When we govern ourselves peacefully, we understand each person's intentions and actions as part of the larger patterns and systems created. Within natural law and ethics, the physical and spiritual are not viewed as separate. Self-governance, in this context, is taught as an extension of self-respect, which in turn becomes respect for "all our relations." Creative power is understood as immanent, as everywhere. Violence is invited when we overstep our place in the natural kinship of all beings and fail to see all the living world as sacred.

Nonviolence is *not a struggle to "seize" power so much as to release it for decentralized use in efficient self-governance.*[13] Decentralization of power—the dispersion or distribution of functions and powers from one central authority to regional and local authorities—can remove authority from dominating, closed systems and return it to an open self. If the open self, many First Nations traditions teach, acts in accord with other systems then harmony can prevail. In open systems *power over* and *power against* can become *power with* or *power through*, as defined above. From this perspective, decentralization can bring power that strengthens. As A.T. Ariyaratne explains: "Decentralization strengthens the centre, really. If the centre has the courage to distribute power, to that extent the centre is strong."[14]

6. Power

In efforts to resist violence and stop injury it is essential to attend to the different forms of power in our world. The Alternatives to Violence Project, begun by The Religious Society of Friends (Quakers) in 1975 in response to requests from prisoners for skills in nonviolent living, developed the following definitions of power (which I have reworked for the purpose of this book):

(1) Power Over

Exploitative: Based on force and usually on society's expectations, open or covert. The powerful make use of others for their own benefit.

Manipulative: Based on persuasion. People influence others for the benefit of themselves.

Competitive: Power *against* others. A one up, one down

THOSE WHO POSSESS THE POWER OF KNOWING AND TRUSTING THEIR MEDICINE GRASP THAT POWER LIGHTLY. THEY UNDERSTAND THAT BY CLUTCHING OR HOLDING ONTO THE *IDEA* OF POWER, ONE BECOMES OBSESSED BY IT.

—JAMIE SAMS

situation; on the positive side, it can test our mettle.

(2) Power With

Nutrient: This power grows from one's care for another, concern for the welfare of another or of a group. The classic example is the power of a parent to nurture a child. Nutrient power may have the negative aspect of paternalism—of doing and deciding things for others that they would be better off doing for themselves.

Shared or conjoined: Comes into being when people join together in a co-operative effort to discover a truth or a path of action to which all can commit themselves sincerely. The effort itself involves honest feedback, sometimes confrontation, and always a sincere respect for the positions of others and a willingness to listen and be convinced when appropriate. It involves both the use and the self-restraint of individual power. Once an understanding is reached, the group can act on it with a power greater than the sum of the individual power of its members. The consensus process at its best produces this result.

Transforming: Power that acts *through* truth, justice and love. This power transcends "human" forms of power. We cannot use it. If we are open to it, it can use us.[15]

Powerlessness occurs when a person is unable to act. It is the loss of self-authority and power within. Powerlessness is not to be confused with passivity. Anne Jones writes of this distinction: "Powerlessness is a political condition, while passivity is a strategy adopted by the powerless to survive."[16] The process of rendering a person powerless is the process of victimization. A victimizer holds *power over* another until the victim is devoid of strength and resources. As Jones explains, "The process of victimization consists of (1) first putting the victim in a position of powerlessness relative to the victimizer, and then (2) repeatedly impressing the victim with his or her powerlessness, including the powerlessness to escape, until the victim adopts passive and compliant behavior to stay alive."[17]

Power within develops through the practise of mindfulness or living with awareness—beginning by being conscious of our breath. Mindfulness is a deep listening to self, to others and to the world. We do this by mercifully turning to what is fearful and bringing careful attention to what is needed to restore inner peace. We care

IF YOU CAN, HELP OTHERS; IF YOU CANNOT DO THAT, AT LEAST DO NOT HARM THEM.

—*DALAI LAMA*

for ourselves and each other by courageously facing whatever is present. *Power within* is inner peace; it is the inherent wholeness and harmlessness of being that resides in each of us.

7. Reciprocity

An ethic of reciprocity guided many cultures before the spirit of nonviolence was eroded by unchecked systems of colonialism and commerce. These systems of patriarchy in most world nation-states are centralized forms of government that have common elements. Hazel Henderson describes patriarchal systems as characterized by hierarchical structures and based on rigid divisions of labor (as well as polarization of sex roles); manipulative technology; instrumentalist, reductionist philosophies; the control of information; and competition both internally and between nations.[18] She says:

> It is, rather, the institutionalization of only the "masculine" value system in the social, institutional, and political spheres and the ghettoizing of the nurturing, co-operative value system within the family and the female roles that are now causing disastrous imbalances. In fact, this insane specialization and division of labor, in which males are supposed to do the thinking, acting, and competing and the females are supposed to do all the feeling and co-operating, has produced severe personal problems for both men and women.[19]

We are left with a world collapsing from unsustainability, inequality and injustice. More and more people suffer psychologically, economically and physically from the loss of home, self-determination and dignity that is the result of any oppressive system based on conquest and exploitation.

We need value systems that will address the power of nurture, redistribution of resources, and our interconnectedness. Great value shifts are occurring; we have at this time an incredible opportunity to redress imbalances and bring forward an ethic of care that has at its centre a generosity of spirit toward all the planet's inhabitants. Principles and practices of nonviolence can be awakened by an ecology of reciprocity which values aligning human actions respectfully with the Earth's natural cycles rather than manipulating natural systems for short-term profit. Henderson succinctly summarizes those principles, which traditions that honor connectedness have kept alive. They are:

WHEN THE HEART IS RIGHT "FOR" AND "AGAINST" ARE FORGOTTEN.
—*THOMAS MERTON*

"COYOTE, DO YOU UNDERSTAND THE THEORY OF RELATIVITY?" "YES, YES I DO. IT'S MUCH EASIER THAT WAY. WHEN I'M HUNGRY I JUST STOP AT ANYONE'S PLACE AND GET A MEAL. YES, IT'S REALLY GOOD TO KNOW WE ARE ALL RELATED."
—*PETER BLUECLOUD*

(1) the value of all human beings;
(2) the right to satisfaction of basic needs (physical, psychological and metaphysical) of all human beings;
(3) equality of opportunity for self-development for all human beings;
(4) recognition that these principles and goals must be achieved within ecological tolerances of lands, seas, air, forests and the total carrying capacity of the biosphere; and
(5) recognition that all these principles apply with equal emphasis to future generations of humans and their biospheric life-support systems, and thus include the respect for all other life-forms and the Earth itself.[20]

8. Sustaining the gaze

KEEP YOUR EYES ON THE PRIZE.
—MARTIN LUTHER KING JR.

It takes great courage not to avert our eyes from the suffering within or around us, and to actively respond. How can we sustain the gaze and look carefully at what is happening in our lives and communities? The pain we inflict or receive through violence is everywhere. Yet we often exist as if there were no pain in the world even when the poverty and suffering in the world is very obvious. Neither apathy nor hysteria will bring us closer to each other in our hopes for change. We need to understand the immense fear and denial in our lives. Joanna Macy believes that beneath this denial and fear is a "notion of the self that our culture has conditioned us to believe through its emphasis on individualism. That view and the way it is conveyed puts a tremendous burden on a person in terms of competition, in terms of defendedness."[21] Defending ourselves from the truths of violence and choosing not to act perpetuates the powerlessness on which violent systems thrive.

WE LEARN WE ARE FREE AS WE BEGIN TO DARE TO ACT NOT AS WE HAVE BEEN TAUGHT THAT WE "SHOULD" BUT—AS THE QUAKERS SAY— ACCORDING TO THE LIGHT THAT IS WITHIN US.
—BARBARA DEMING

What is becoming clearer is that we are called to work on the self and find those places that inspire compassion and even joy in personal, local and global healing. As Macy says, we can "be invited to come home to the way of participation in this world, knowing we are part of the web of life, which in our heart of hearts is what we want most."[22]

Fundamentalism, particularly patristic and nationalist forms, prevents generosity of spirit and apportionment of resources. To assume the superiority of one religion, economy, gender or politic in righteous power over another is to reduce life experience to a single interpretation that denies and eventually destroys the multiplicity and diversity we need to survive. It is important that our gaze not become fixed in identifying ourselves as the victim or violator, so that we miss the powerful and peaceful potential of our true selves.

We can become fundamentalists as nonviolent activists if we corner nonviolence into unalterable definitions and strategies. If we open up the principles and axioms of nonviolence we discover the process is ongoing and derived more from fluid strength of heart than frozen perfection of action. Nonviolence finds its power in relatedness and diversity rather than ideological authoritarianism. In our relatedness and creative will there is the potential for endless possibilities of peaceful change.

SELF HAS MANY FACES. VICTIM AND TYRANT BOTH SUFFER. ALIENATION TAKES MANY FORMS, INCLUDING GREED, JEALOUSLY, SEXUAL OBSESSION, RIGHTEOUSNESS, ANGER, HATRED, HYPOCRISY AND OTHER FORMS OF ACUTE CONFUSION. SUFFERING'S FACE IS ABUSER AND ABUSED.

—JOAN HALIFAX

9. Nonviolent strategy

Traditionally, nonviolent action is developed through tactical strategy. Pam McAllister has summarized three categories of nonviolent action that theorist Gene Sharp outlined in his work, *The Politics of Nonviolent Action*:

> The first is nonviolent protest and persuasion. With actions we name what we think is wrong, point our fingers at it and try to help others understand. This category would include such tactics as petitioning, picketing, demonstrating and lobbying.
>
> The second category is nonviolent non-co-operation. With these actions we deliberately fold our hands and turn our backs, refusing to participate in the wrong we have named. This category would include such tactics as boycotts, strikes and tax resistance.
>
> The third category is nonviolent intervention. With these actions we face the wrong we have named, the wrong we have refused to aid, and we step into the way, interfere, block. This category would include such tactics as physical obstruction, blockades, civil disobedience and sit-ins.[23]

NONVIOLENCE DOESN'T ALWAYS WORK—BUT VIOLENCE NEVER DOES.

—MADGE MICHAELS

Notes

[1] Adrienne Rich, *Blood, Bread and Poetry: Selected Prose* (New York: W.W. Norton & Company, 1986), p. 145.

[2] Ibid., p. 144.

[3] Ibid.

[4] Jack Kornfield, *A Path With Heart* (New York: Bantam Books, 1993), pp. 26-27.

[5] As quoted in Thomas Merton, ed., *Gandhi on Non-Violence* (New York: New Directions, 1964), p. 28. From M.K. Gandhi, *Non-Violence in Peace and War* (Ahmedabad: Navajivan Publishing House, 1948), Vol. II, p. 34.

[6] M.K. Gandhi, *Satyragraha* (Ahmedabad: Navajivan Publishing House, 1951), p. 384.

[7] Merton, *Gandhi on Non-Violence*, p. 35.

[8] Ibid., p. 23.

[9] This book cannot begin to adequately discuss the traditional significance of the power of nonviolence through strategies of political ju-jitsu. In Richard Gregg's political maxim, *The Power of Nonviolence*, first published in 1935, there is an excellent discussion of moral ju-jitsu.

[10] "How Nonviolent Struggle Works" (Cambridge, MA.: The Albert Einstein Institute).

[11] Similar also to Taichi Ch'uan. Thanks to Doug Woolidge's translation of Master Wu Kongstau's writings on Wu style Taichi Ch'uan, p.1. Gabriola Island, BC, unpublished.

[12] Judith Plant, "A Conversation with Marie Wilson," in *Healing the Wounds: The Promise of Ecofeminism*, ed. Judith Plant (Philadelphia & Gabriola Island: New Society Publishers, 1989), p. 215.

[13] Joanna Macy, *Despair and Personal Power in the Nuclear Age* (Philadelphia & Gabriola Island: New Society Publishers, 1983), p. 34.

[14] Catherine Ingram, *In The Footsteps of Gandhi: Conversations with Spiritual Social Activists* (Berkeley, CA: Parallax Press, 1990), p. 136.

[15] Alternatives to Violence Project, *Second Level Manual*, Section F (New York, 1990 edition), pp. 14-15.

[16] Anne Jones, *Next Time She'll Be Dead: Battering and How to Stop It* (Boston: Beacon Press, 1994), p. 181.

[17] Ibid.

[18] Hazel Henderson, *The Politics of the Solar Age: Alternatives to Economics* (Indiana: Knowledge Systems, 1988), p. 364.

[19] Ibid., p. 366.

[20] Ibid., p. 386.

[21] Macy, *Despair and Personal Power*, p. 164.

[22] Ibid., p. 165.

[23] In *You Can't Kill the Spirit*, p.9.

OUR WORK

IV   TRUTH AND TESTIMONY

1. Breaking the silence

THE FIRST DISCOVERY, OPENING TO WHAT WE KNOW AND FEEL, TAKES COURAGE. LIKE GANDHI'S SATYAGRAHA, IT INVOLVES "TRUTH-FORCE." PEOPLE ARE NOT GOING TO FIND THEIR TRUTH-FORCE OR INNER AUTHORITY IN LISTENING TO THE EXPERTS, BUT IN LISTENING TO THEMSELVES, FOR EVERYONE IN HER OR HIS WAY IS AN EXPERT ON WHAT IT IS LIKE TO LIVE ON AN ENDANGERED PLANET.

—JOANNA MACY

There are many amongst us who are condemned to silence, who fear for their lives, who fear reprisal for speaking, who are coerced and forced into silence. All over the world women are breaking that silence which shrouds the conditions of women's lives. We are liberating lives for too long legislated, penalized, distorted and censored by others.

This is a testimony of self where before many were convinced there was no self, and it is a telling of the circumstances in which women's lives are forced into conditions they do not want or chose. For this telling to happen we need to ensure our voice is determined by the body of knowledge and inquiry coming from within—a voice belonging to none other than she who lives it. From this place of authenticity women are building a community of voices *that in its hearing* allows us glimpses into the possibilities of freedom, joy and transformation.

The telling is not easy, for the obstacles and the threats against telling are many. Finding our way out of *the overwhelmingness of the dominant* requires stepping through walls of fear.[1] There are silences, Robin Morgan describes, that *will not speak* and there are silences that *may not speak*. The first explodes, the second implodes in violence. There is another place though, even in her fear, where a woman discovers "her silence is within her power to break, even if his violence is not. Silence is the first thing within the power of the enslaved to shatter. From that shattering, everything else spills forward."[2]

This other place where *everything else spills forward* is a place where our intelligence resists the loss of consciousness and steps outside the vault of violence. A place where we learn the value of defining, discussing and sharing the difficulties and joys of our lives. By breaking our silences we build strength in the stories of healing and bear testimony to a nonviolent life too long hidden from view. We begin with the stories of our own lives, including the stories of when we were silenced.

2. Telling our stories

Story-telling has been an enduring part of human lives. Story-telling brings attention to the realities of our lives. Stories can serve to inform, connect and release us. Story-telling, if done consciously, brings self-knowledge and self-acceptance. By telling our stories, we can take back what has been shamed, disowned and lessened. We define our lives for ourselves and bring into light what has been hidden, denied and lied about.

THE UNIVERSE IS MADE OF STORIES, NOT OF ATOMS.
—MURIEL RUKEYSER

Our stories serve us and this planet by their power of exposing and protecting. Writing about the power of our stories, Joan Halifax says that "like our immune systems they defend us and the people against attacks of debilitating alienation."[3] We tell stories out of a hope that we will go on, and as a way back to a birthright of healing and wholeness. Like Sheherazade in *The Arabian Nights* we tell our stories to save ourselves and the world we love.[4]

Telling our stories requires more love than logic. It requires the willingness to embrace whatever is there. We give voice to the unnameable before it destroys us. Our stories are the roots that enable our growth; no part of our life is unusable. All that we feel and know can help to locate the truth of our lives. By disclosing the events in our lives we can give birth to the full reality of who we are. Understanding the fullness of our anger and longing for joy motivates necessary change.

THE STORIES WE TELL OURSELVES, PARTICULARLY THE SILENT OR BARELY AUDIBLE ONES, ARE VERY POWERFUL. ONE MUST OPEN THE WINDOW TO SEE THEM, THE DOOR TO POSSIBILITY.
—SUSAN GRIFFIN

Repeated tellings are revealing. In the retelling, the geography of our lives shows itself again and again, often revealing deeper truths each time. Our stories can eventually make room for our shadows and secrets, bringing oxygen to that which literally makes us sick. We can nurse our stories by treating them like holy patients. In the details of our suffering and searching we find what needs tending and how our life-journey is taking shape.

Our stories create a home for those experiences and feelings that have been exiled, and in this home we can care for our souls. Our stories provide places of reference in the work of reshaping the spiritual and political contexts of our lives. They are the bridge we walk on in our journey from exile to existence, and violence to nonviolence. By telling our stories we create for ourselves and our community a listening that is essential to existing together. We testify and listen to the suffering and recovery that many experience and through these acts of testimony and witnessing we bring sanity to reality.

3. Fair witnessing

THERE ARE TWO MEANINGS OF THE WORD "WITNESS": TO STAND AND BE COUNTED, AND TO BE AN EYE-WITNESS OF OTHERS' LIVES AND EXPERIENCES AND SUFFERINGS IN RELATION TO ONE'S OWN.

—*WITNESS FOR PEACE*

Listening to another person's story is a form of witnessing that is often missing in our lives. Being witnesses to each others' stories allows us to overcome the isolation often engendered in abusive relationships and fractured communities. If we are to be whole, we must listen fairly, without blocking or forcing another person's words. By fully listening to the wounded and wounder in our communities or to those aspects of ourselves that have been rejected, we help to break the "conspiracy of silence" that has been the greatest barrier to recovery.[5]

Bearing witness to one another's testimonies makes life more lucid. And with lucidity our inner life is revealed. We make official the unofficial stories. Susan Griffin helps us understand this:

> It is a method used now to heal the survivors of sexual abuse and torture. The survivor tells the story of suffering over and over to a listener who will hear and respond to all that happened. The compassion of the listener is crucial. Is this because part of the trauma is the cruelty and coldness of the perpetrator? The survivor has been humiliated and blamed as well as physically wounded. The one who listens provides an accepting field for the story. An essential dimension. Moment by moment we help each other to see.[6]

EVERY STORY HAS A SACRED DIMENSION NOT SO MUCH BECAUSE GODS ARE CENTRAL IN THEM BUT BECAUSE A PERSON'S SENSE OF SELF AND THE WORLD IS CREATED THROUGH HIS/HER STORY.

—*THOMAS MOORE*

Compassionate listening helps another *hear themselves into being*.[7] To take the risk to speak from the heart, particularly when a story has already been refused a hearing or subverted into silence, requires a listener who is hearing with his or her own heart.

Many stories of abuse and war have been denied hearings. The Vietnam War uncovered a pattern of military cover-up that is habitual to many governments. The "official" story often distorts what has really happened. Most official stories are told by men and exclude women's experiences. Consequently, whole centuries of women's stories are missing. This exclusion aims to destroy those "feminine" qualities in men and women that are most needed in an interactive and fair world system based on an ethic of care. Such an imbalance tragically undermines a healthy dialectic between men and women. By finding our voices we can reshape a dialectic that is fluid, open and deeply mindful of the fragility of life.

The battered women's movement showed remarkable courage as victims who survived male violence began to speak publicly about their torment despite threats of murder and the fear of not being believed. The sickness of secrecy kills people daily. At its worst, it is a form of terrorism. It is this pattern we must change. *People can handle the truth,* Anne Wilson Schaef wrote. *It's the illusions that are difficult.*[8]

> THE WOMAN POET GREW SILENT FOR THOUSANDS OF YEARS. MEN TOOK EXCLUSIVE CHARGE OF WHAT HAD BEEN THE OFFICE OF WOMEN. THEY EXTOLLED THE MOON AND LOVE.
> —CHRISTA WOLF

4. Defying conventional wisdom

Stories of nonviolence are also often missing in our lives. We need to tell and hear stories of courage that defy conventional thinking about human strength. Nonviolent stories can remind us of what is possible when we look deeply into our hearts during times of danger. They can be life-affirming devices that keep our hearts eternally open to the strength we normally don't recognize. Within the tradition of story-telling, the potential of nonviolence can literally come alive and the power of love and peacemaking can be shared right in the moment.

Without personal articulation we are prevented from grasping our own nuances and reflecting on the many points of view our experiences offer. Healing is possible when we avoid the fundamentalism of truth and instead, search for insight gained by finding many meanings to our stories. It is through insight that we can rescue our stories, frozen in a single meaning or convention. A person's truth can have many meanings. When we approach our lives with an investigative curiosity and openness, we find truths that deepen and evolve in their meaning. Recognizing the continuous unfolding of our minds, we are able to see our lives for the endurance and diversity they bring.

> WE LONG FOR THE TRUTH IN ALL ITS CONTRADICTIONS.
> —RITA DOVE

If we speak from our hearts of the living conditions of our bodies—our true texts of revelation—we begin the work of healing separation and living in wholeness. Our revelations then can take us outside the narrow confines of cultural convention into wider spheres of understanding and possibility. There are many women and men who, in daily living, are taking care not to harm, who are choosing not to ignore those in need, and who are not hiding behind privilege. We need those stories too.

> WE MUST CARE FOR THE TRUTH IN FRONT OF US MORE THAN CONSISTENCY.
> —MAHATMA GANDHI

5. An ethic of care

We can work together to prevent violence in our homes and communities. We can all begin by choosing not to lie about violence to ourselves and our children. When we hide or distort truths about violence we perpetuate the conspiracy of silence that puts a stranglehold on necessary learning, just action and healing. We need to learn what prevents abusive behavior and find ways to be part of the prevention.

THERE IS NO HEALING ALTERNATIVE TO RECOGNIZING AND FACING THE TRUTH.
—ALICE MILLER

We need to continue to build an ethic of care that respects, from the day our children are born, the freedom of discovery they need, in homes where caretakers are calm, safe and unconditionally loving. Our children need a pace of living that allows them to grow gently into themselves and their gifts. They need to be protected from forms of pressure and noise that are stressful for their minds and bodies. Our children are often overstimulated, rushed and not fully listened to. More than anything, they need to know they matter, that every child is worth being listened to and their ideas worth talking about. We need to do whatever we can to secure environments for our children that are relaxed and supportive.

This is difficult and often impossible for those parents living in conditions of poverty, who suffer from lack of choice, of day care, from low self-esteem and exhaustion—women and men who have never known the luxury of choice, the privilege of education, the abundance of food or the security of a sufficient pay cheque or affordable health insurance. An ethic of care requires we address concretely the conditions of illiteracy, privilege, of class, race and oppression.

IT IS THE TRUTH THAT SETS US FREE AND THE TRUTH IS THAT WE, WHO ARE ALL PART OF ONE ANOTHER, CANNOT LIVE WITHOUT THE WHOLE LIVES TO WHICH NATURE CALLS.
—BARBARA DEMING

This requires we role-model non-discriminatory and inclusive definitions of family. There are families where fathers are allies to women and children and actively work for the happiness and independence of the females in their lives, fathers who actively are part of the physical and psychic care of their children—who learn to provide the tenderness of warmth and closeness all children need to survive, men who gently teach their sons that sexual violence is unmanly and cowardly, that no man is "entitled" to sex, and that every boy and man must learn the meaning of consent and sexual intimacy without control.

There are also families of women and men in same-sex relationships who need to be recognized as being legitimate and entitled to be visible and supported in their care for each other and their children. There are mothers who encourage looking at other women as role models to expand the options in their daughters' lives and teach survival skills that increase self-esteem and self-awareness. And there are extended families where grandparents, other relatives and friends are welcomed and encouraged as caregivers who are active in the well-being and education of children they know.

6. The need for education

Our children depend on us for knowledge that deepens the capacity to love without fear, prejudice and violence. Our boys need to learn to be anti-rapist and our girls to be self-determining. This begins with teaching how the current socialization of men and women has created a predator-prey dynamic that depends on thinking and acting violently and submissively. We can alert our children that socialization and gender stereotyping that shape one's development through messages of sexism and the superiority of one person over another are unacceptable. No one need be defined in a female or male role that is given a status of inferiority. The alternatives, our children need to know, are not only life-affirming, they are life-saving.

TRUTH EMERGES FROM BALANCE.
—*I Ching*

With our teenagers we must finds ways to replace sexual ignorance with sexual knowledge. Ignorance is not bliss; it is debilitating. Until our girls and boys are well aware of their physiology and reproduction, they will not be sexually responsible or have the knowledge they need to make informed and principled decisions. For teenagers to grow into lives of dignity and self-worth, their dignity and self-worth must be affirmed and supported. If we are proactive we find ways to reinforce their individual strengths and honor their self-determination.

We help our children grow into healthy adults when we avoid imposing gender stereotypes and emphasize instead, qualities that strengthen their humanity. If we want confident and caring children we must find ways of making this possible. In Emilie Buchwald's wonderful essay, "Raising Girls for the 21st Century," she explains clearly:

'TIS NOT REVELATION WE NEED BUT THE UNCLOUDING OF OUR EYES.
—*Emily Dickinson*

> A general recognition is dawning that our culture will need both women and men who are strong, wise, and generous if the future is to be better than the present. The nurture and education of girls must emphasize the importance of their role in that future.

What a girl wants, what a woman wants, is what Freud knew is held precious by every man: self-determination, autonomy within reason, life without undue fear, liberty without causing harm to others, and the ability to pursue one's happiness. None of those desires can be fulfilled for women so long as we live in a rape culture.[9]

7. The need to challenge

WHEREAS
LANGUAGE AND
NAMING ARE
POWER, SILENCE
IS OPPRESSION
—IS VIOLENCE.
—ADRIENNE RICH

We need to continue to challenge and change (1) the cultural training that institutionalizes gender inequity and sexual stereotyping, (2) complicity with a rape culture through a refusal to inform ourselves about the reality of rape, (3) the consolidation and use of power that is preoccupied with profit and domination, and (4) the lies generated when we do nothing to counter the realities of our lives, in which violence is condoned.

Education can release our ignorance and spark a commitment to change which, in this generation, can transform violence. The changes confronting us require a revision and reconfiguration of power, which some of us will find difficult and painful. But the benefits are far-reaching and the possibilities of a world in which life is truly loved are limitless. When everyone's story is freed from its place of exile and cherished for the gifts it contributes to the liberation of truth and transformation, we will know we are well on our way.

Notes

[1] Tillie Olsen, *Silences* (New York: Dell Publishing Co., 1978), p. 256.

[2] Robin Morgan, *The Demon Lover: On the Sexuality of Terrorism* (New York: W.W. Norton & Company, 1989), p. 322.

[3] Joan Halifax, *The Fruitful Darkness: Reconnecting with the Body of the Earth* (Harper: San Francisco, 1993), p. 104.

[4] I am indebted to Susan Griffin for this line. Please see *A Chorus of Stones* (New York: Doubleday, 1992), p. 363.

[5] The term "conspiracy of silence" came from the important work of Sandra Butler on incest, titled *Conspiracy of Silence: The Trauma of Incest* (San Francisco: Volcano Press, 1985 [updated]).

[6] Ibid., Susan Griffin, p. 298.

[7] The work of Nelle Morton, particularly the essay "The Word We Cannot Yet Speak" included in her book *The Journey is Home* (Boston: Beacon Press, 1985), explores the fullness of this process.

[8] Anne Wilson Schaef, *Beyond Therapy, Beyond Science* (New York: Harper Collins, 1992), p. 284.

[9] In *Transforming a Rape Culture* (Minneapolis: Milkweed Publications, 1994), ed. Buchwald, Fletcher and Roth, p. 181.

V SAFETY AND SANCTUARY

1. The battered women's movement

Violence in women's lives was largely hidden and private before the emergence of the battered women's movement. It has been as the result of the battered women's movement that battery and abuse have been named, brought to public attention, and sanctuary and services provided for families at risk. Because of its grassroots beginnings in the larger women's movement, there are numerous pioneers who "mothered" this movement into a reality in which the lives of many women, men and children were and are being recovered with dignity.

This is a movement that, in the face of social indifference, disbelief and backlash, has built on the ingenuity and strength of grassroots collectivism, and feminist world revisioning. This revisioning recognized and called for institutional change that focuses on the material conditions necessary for women to realize full independence and equality as world citizens. These conditions include housing, child care, education, adequate wages, sufficient welfare benefits, job training and affirmative action programs. The battered women's movement also changed the terms of social response to violence in ways that enabled women to receive care that was not entrenched in traditional and exploitative therapies. These therapies often perpetuated the denial and shroud of silence covering men's violence. The battered women's movement encouraged surviving victims to reconstruct their lives so they were not forced into roles of powerlessness and victimization—a response focused on both the individual and collective strength of private and political change.

In the earlier stages of the movement, abused women "were not the *clients* that they are today but active participants in a joint struggle."[1] It is not uncommon today to see more and more private and profit-oriented therapists working as "experts" outside, and sometimes hostile to, action-oriented community-based groups.

Non-profit organizations have suffered from the reactionary backlash created by right-wing governments, state-defined services, negative stereotyping of feminists, and the "professionalism" of work that is removed from the context of community and issues of race and class.

The split between those who see violence against women as a political and social issue and those who see it only as an individual problem has created challenging differences inside and outside the movement since the early '80s.[2] As Susan Schechter warned us in 1982, unless the politically constructed origins of violence against women are acknowledged in an encompassing response to that violence then "battered women will disappear again—their plight reprivatized."[3]

As with so many grassroots movements, the battered women's movement grew out of volunteer work and the contributions of women in their own communities who, with little or no money, organized safe houses, shelters, advocacy, criminal justice reform and anti-violence education programs. Numerous women, moved by the pragmatic generosity of community-based care and the insights of radical feminism, recognized fully how the personal and political significance of violence against women were inseparable. As summarized by Ron Thorne-Finch:

> It eventually coalesced into a diversified, social, political, and economic force for change. Within a few years, there accumulated a momentum strong enough to begin shifting our well-entrenched understanding and preferred treatment of male violence against women from the physiological and intrapsychic toward the social constructionist. Women had succeeded at socially defining an existing condition (male violence against women) and its origins (social constructionism), and made it more difficult for either to remain ignored.[4]

The proliferation of services and policy reform in the 1970s and 1980s would have been impossible without a feminist political presence.[5] Central to successful organizing of support services and criminal justice reform was the concentration of small local groups that linked through larger networking activity. On both local and national levels, issues of racism and class were addressed and continue to be today. Coalitions around the world continue the unfinished work of advocating for societies that are free of the domination and dependence found in abusive families and in socio-economic systems that prevent egalitarianism and self-determination.

THE FULL AND EFFECTIVE PROMOTION OF WOMEN'S RIGHTS CAN BEST OCCUR IN CONDITIONS OF INTERNATIONAL PEACE AND SECURITY.
—*ADVANCEMENT OF WOMEN, PARA. 13*

The battered women's movement has had to work simultaneously on many fronts. Through broad-based organizing, the differing needs of battered women have taught women the necessity of learning to hear each woman's reality and actively learn to educate ourselves about the differences in our lives. This motivated the movement to welcome diversity and celebrate difference. Honoring difference teaches women to respond to abused women in ways that genuinely respect the uniqueness of each woman's historical and cultural conditions.

Through its organizing efforts the battered women's movement has irreversibly changed public consciousness about the lives of abused women, the myth of the family as "always a safe haven from a brutal world," and has led to the provision of services and sanctuary for many in need built on a model of empowerment.[6] Susan Schechter has carefully documented the significance of a movement that has created a vision of a better life for all.

> The contributions of the battered women's movement involve not only content, but process as well. Its use of feminist self-help as both a service and a political strategy continues a tradition followed within the women's movement and offers important insights for future political activity. Self-help validates non-hierarchical, non-professional service models as the most effective form of helping battered women.[7]

2. The politics of safety

Leaving a relationship doesn't always mean the abuse stops, nor should a woman be expected to leave her home in order for help to be provided for herself and her children. Yet, it is often the woman who is forced to leave. Until an abusing man takes full responsibility for his violence and is actively getting help in ways that are accountable, observable and positive, the abuse usually continues, if not with his current partner then with the next. The violence will often escalate, if not in the home, then outside of it, particularly in the form of harassment, stalking and threats. And so women and children, refugees of a domestic war, take cover by the thousands in houses and centres that are places of protection.

When the right to sanctuary inside and outside the home is violated then the severance of this liberty becomes very political. Politicians must clearly acknowledge the human rights violations committed in the home and make men's violence an issue of national security. John Stoltenberg's work for specific policy change and campaigns against violence against women fervently questions this lack of political action and projects the possibility of something different:

> Imagine candidates stumping for public office debating how best to stop rape. Imagine them inspiring us with new ideas and new programs to eliminate crimes of sexual violence completely. Imagine them promising bold and innovative leadership to set a national priority to "demoralize" rape, to refute myths about rape through all the mass media, to educate young people about personal rights and bodily integrity throughout the public school system, to create a national climate of opinion in which ending rape matters—because it gets talked about and cared about and people take it seriously. Even among groups of men there would emerge a new kind of peer pressure, discouraging rape rather than encouraging it, labelling coercive sex as one of the most not-cool things a guy could do. Imagine a candidate declaring on national television, "As president, I will commit the resources of my administration to making the United States a rape-free zone."[8]

Intervention begins with assuring protection to victims of violence and holding offenders responsible. With safety, a victim can begin the journey of returning to a self that doesn't live in a state of seige. Across North America, shelters for battered women and children are full of families beginning this healing. They arose out of the direct need, as refugee camps have, for those caught between a zone of war and homelessness. Most battered women must leave their homes to find safety. Very few perpetrators are removed unless the violence has already caused visible injury or members of his family are found dead.

"The politics of safety," Michael Kimmel writes, "may be the missing link in the transformation of men's lives, in their capacity for change." Safety, he tells us, is

> more than the absence of danger, although that wouldn't be such a bad thing in itself. Safety is pro-active, the creation of space in which all people, women and men, gay and straight, and of all colors, can experience and express the fullness of their beings.[9]

The fullness of our beings. To allow expression of the fullness of our beings in right relationship to ourselves and each other, we must restructure what safety is and whose responsibility it is to ensure safety exists.

WHEN PATRIARCHAL MAN'S DEEP-SEATED FEARS OF THE ELEMENTAL POWER OF THE FEMALE, HIS OWN BODY, AND HIS EMOTIONS ARE INDULGED...BY A SUPPOSEDLY STRONG LEADER CALLING FOR EVEN MORE INTENSELY PATRIARCHAL SOCIAL STRUCTURES, FASCISM CAN RESULT.... DESIRE BECOMES MUTATED INTO DESIRE FOR VIOLENCE AGAINST DESIRE.... FASCISM IS A SET OF VIOLENT FANTASIES AND ACTS MEANT TO PROTECT (PATRIARCHAL) MAN FROM HIS BODY, HIS DESIRES, HIS EMOTIONS, AND HIS IMMEDIATE LOCAL RELATIONS WITH OTHER PEOPLE.
—CHARLENE SPRETNAK

3. Defining consent

Teaching ourselves and our children about what constitutes sexual consent is a step toward safety. Much of the long-term injury incurred from child sexual assault is the complex confusion arising from sexual touch and arousal that occurs before one has the capacity to choose and determine what is safe. Unless the right to a self-determined sexuality is learned in an environment of unqualified respect and safety, then violation is likely to occur. The protection of these rights must be taken seriously by all the systems that shape our lives.

LEARN TO LOOK WITH AN EQUAL EYE, UPON ALL BEINGS,/ SEEING THE ONE SELF IN ALL.

—SRIMAD BHAGAVATUM

Any form of unwelcomed or uninvited sex is assault, no matter the circumstances. Sex between an adult and a child defies consent. Knowing what constitutes a violation is as important as knowing what feels like a violation. The only way to prevent rape is to be fully conscious of the other person's humanity. We can choose to honor this humanity, the body's vulnerability and the soul's beauty, by sharing sexual pleasure with only those who treat us with respect. When two people are wide awake and devoted to an intimacy that is determined by respect, then many precautions against violation are put into place.

The creation of consent and setting of limits is often seen as women's responsibility. With one's eye only on women's behavior, the avoidance of the inequality and bias inherent in our culture is revealed. This is a bias and often, a hatred, that feeds rape. We are all affected by belief systems based on odious distortions about women's sexual availability. Many of these distortions blind us to

THE HUMAN SHAPE IS A GHOST/ MADE OF DISTRACTION AND PAIN./ SOMETIMES PURE LIGHT, SOMETIMES CRUEL,/ TRYING WILDLY TO OPEN,/ THIS IMAGE TIGHTLY HELD WITHIN ITSELF.

—RUMI

the shared responsibility for consent. Anytime there is a sense of *sexual entitlement*, the predatory nature of aggressive sex begins its abusive course of action. In the essay "Conversations of Consent," Michael Biernbaum and Joseph Weinberg describe the victim-blaming arising from such distortions:

> The old saw "She got herself raped" reveals the operating paradigm: it's all *her* responsibility to say "no" and to attempt to set *my* limits. Rape occurs when *she* doesn't succeed. This is an analysis that is familiar to many men and women whose victim-blaming usually revolves around this point. The process of consent seeks to redress this disastrous imbalance, charging men with the responsibility for our behavior and for respecting the integrity of our partner.[10]

Victim-blaming has created impossible situations for women where consent between sexual partners is not explicit, verbal or shared. Consent is not present unless we are certain that (1) what we are doing is not felt as a violation, (2) at all times sex is welcomed, (3) both partners are free to change their minds, to say what is needed, to share control of the situation, and not feel pressured.[11] This is a conversation and process that occurs with mindfulness and dignity, not by "forcing a woman to have sex when she says no, conniving, coercing, pushing, ignoring efforts to get you to stop, getting her so drunk that she loses the ability (or consciousness) that one needs to give consent."[12]

What was once defined as male sexual etiquette is now often known as date rape. It will not be possible to ignore the full reality of rape if we learn a kind of "sexual democracy" where we celebrate eroticism and so revere our bodies and spirits.

ONLY WHEN WE HAVE ALTERNATIVES TO VIOLENCE AND THE THREAT TO VIOLENCE FOR SETTLING CONFLICTS WILL WE BE TRULY SECURE.
—WOMEN'S PEACE PRESENCE

4. Self-defence

When sexual intimacy is not honored—and there are those who understand consent and will still rape—then other tools for increasing personal safety are needed. It would help our children if these tools were taught in all schools and affirmed as possible, but not guaranteed, forms of protection. Basically, self-defence begins with the belief system that our lives are worth caring for. Self-defence is about planning, exercising judgment, learning to identify early warning signals and threatening situations and to take responsibility for one's safety. Self-defence also means challenging beliefs about femininity that keep women powerless.[13]

Self-defence classes teach students how to watch for danger and if possible, how not to move into the danger of an exploitative or coercive situation. Students learn to identify predatory behavior and signs of danger. Self-defence involves refusing to keep our girls passive, by teaching assertiveness. This is assertiveness that not only helps girls learn how to define for themselves their sexual desire but also how to hold others accountable for abusive behavior.

IF THE FIRST WOMAN GOD EVER MADE WAS STRONG ENOUGH TO TURN THE WORLD UPSIDE DOWN, THEN WOMEN TOGETHER OUGHT TO BE ABLE TO TURN IT RIGHT SIDE UP AGAIN.
—SOJOURNER TRUTH

Learning self-defence deepens self-awareness. We learn to trust ourselves by listening to our inner voices, paying attention to body sensations that can alert us to our fear, discomfort or confusion. Self-defence teaches specific forms of non-co-operation and non-compliance when a person's needs and safety aren't honored. Wendo is a traditional form of self-defence designed for increasing, in girls, the confidence in and consciousness of their body strength, and their capacity for resolute resistance in the face of an attacker.

5. Zones of peace

Safety in our society also involves the offering of sanctuary. The sanctuary movement in North America was given birth by religious groups and individuals responding to the need of millions of Central Americans displaced by war, many of whom were denied asylum in the United States because of U.S. military involvement in their homelands. Throughout history, numerous underground railroads have transported hunted Jews, enslaved Africans, Latin American refugees, war fugitives, draft dodgers, battered women and abused children to safety. Bringing sanctuary to individuals has meant, for many, opening one's door in the face of systemic oppression and threat of imprisonment. For those seeking refuge it is life-saving.

In the early '70s, the battered women's movement began a grassroots network of "safe houses" where women, fleeing from men's violence, could find safety for themselves and their children in another person's home. These houses were anonymous to the public but well-known to those working to free women from violence. The immense need for safety that was demonstrated through the endless use of safe houses gave rise to the establishment of larger shelters or transition houses where many thousands of women and children are given sanctuary yearly. What was once invisible to many women not so long ago is now more accessible.

It is a deep sharing of one's resources, national and personal, that makes possible the transition from danger to safety. Unless safety is provided, many women are trapped in dangerous circumstances. The presence of sanctuary in our communities, whether a safe house or a battered woman's shelter, is an active practice of nonviolence that has saved many lives from the risk of homicide and suicide.

Sanctuaries provide safety as well as an opportunity to build alliances. Alliance-building breaks through isolation and separateness. By being allies who promise no harm, we create zones of peace. A safe place, however, does not bring permanent safety from violence. Real change in our responses to violence against women takes place when we also develop sanctuary within ourselves and encourage whole communities to become zones of peace.

WE ARE THE
MIRROR AS WELL AS
THE FACE IN IT./
WE ARE TASTING
THE TASTE
THIS MINUTE/
OF ETERNITY.
WE ARE PAIN/
AND WHAT CURES
PAIN, BOTH.
WE ARE/
THE SWEET, COLD
WATER AND THE JAR
THAT POURS.

—Rumi

PERHAPS, FINALLY,
WE CAN TRUST A
LITTLE MORE—BOTH
OURSELVES AND THE
PROCESS. WE HAVE
MUCH MORE TO
OFFER THAN WE
MAY REALIZE. ALL
WE HAVE TO DO IS
ASK, "HOW CAN I
HELP?" WITH AN
OPEN HEART, AND
THEN REALLY LISTEN.

—Ram Dass

6. Inner sanctuary

The development of sanctuary in our lives can be related to the nonviolence practice of *ahimsa*. In a positive Western context, ahimsa means dynamic compassion. The development of sanctuaries or peace zones in ourselves and in our communities requires immense compassion. Sanctuary is related to ahimsa and compassion because the offering of safe homes teaches a loving engagement with those around us. Nathaniel Altman explains:

> The teaching of ahimsa represents the essence of reverence for life to be applied in every facet of daily existence, and represents a creative involvement in life and its movement. Far from advocating the adoption of an escapist lifestyle, the true understanding of dynamic compassion encourages us to joyously accept personal responsibility to respect life and further it as much as possible. Ahimsa stresses positive action.... Ahimsa can be called the dynamic expression of compassion and truth in some of the most difficult and dangerous situations.[14]

Compassion "is not pity," Matthew Fox writes, "but a genuine love for all our relations, a love of our shared interdependence."[15] Sanctuary is the result of such love. Sanctuaries help our communities become open systems. Communities which respond to the needs of those suffering from violence, including those charged with assault, do not turn their backs on suffering. Creative community responses to the suffering of our neighbors is a necessary step toward nonviolent transformation.

It is as important to find sanctuary in ourselves as it is to offer it to others. Finding sanctuary in ourselves can take many forms. Prayer, retreat, silence, worship, a walk in the woods, reading and conscious rest are all examples of sanctuary we can give to ourselves. In our everyday lives, we need time-outs for renewal as our lives are often full of compulsive behaviors. Many of us need to learn to rest with the conscious intention of creating moments of inner peace or grace. This can bring strength to our relationships with others. Providing times for inner sanctuary in our lives helps our children also develop practices of generosity and peace that can benefit themselves and others.

It is helpful to create places of quiet in our homes. This could be a meditation room or a corner of a room where it is understood that one can sit quietly and simply breathe. Consciously focusing on our breath can quickly reduce agitation. Thich Nhat Hahn

YOU MUST HAVE A ROOM OR A CERTAIN HOUR OF THE DAY OR SO WHERE YOU DO NOT KNOW WHAT WAS IN THE MORNING PAPER; WHERE YOU DO NOT KNOW WHO YOUR FRIENDS ARE; YOU DON'T KNOW WHAT YOU OWE ANYBODY, OR WHAT THEY OWE YOU—BUT A PLACE WHERE YOU SIMPLY EXPERIENCE AND BRING FORTH WHAT YOU ARE, AND WHAT YOU MIGHT BE.... AT FIRST YOU MAY FIND NOTHING'S HAPPENING.... BUT IF YOU HAVE A SACRED PLACE AND USE IT, TAKE ADVANTAGE OF IT, SOMETHING WILL HAPPEN.

—JOSEPH CAMPBELL

describes this practice in his books, *Being Peace* and *Peace in Every Step*. Focusing on our breath and sitting quietly every morning with our children in a special place, he teaches, is a gentle way of bringing calm. *It is in itself, a powerful peace education.*

Zones of peace in ourselves and in our communities can develop a simplicity of being. The simpler the effort—be it a quiet space in our hearts, a meditation corner, a spare room—the more possible it is. Is this kind of simplicity difficult because simplicity has become unfamiliar in our complex consumer societies and may feel abnormal to some of us? Can we take up a practice of simplicity that permits a quietening in the mind and a safe place for our hearts? Can we find these zones of peace, religious and secular, that support a spirit of sanctuary whether we are an inmate in a prison, a woman in a transition house, a parent with many children, an administrator with many responsibilities?

THESE ARE THE THINGS WE PRAYED FOR: CHILDREN, ELDERS, SICK PEOPLE, PEOPLE IN PRISON AND PEACE.
—*ELIZABETH LITTLE ELK*

Notes

[1] Susan Schechter, *Women and Male Violence: The Visions and Struggles of the Battered Women's Movement* (Boston: South End Press, 1982), p. 4.

[2] Ibid., see p. 311-321.

[3] Ibid., p. 314.

[4] *Ending The Silence: The Origins and Treatment of Male Violence Against Women and Children* (Toronto: University of Toronto, 1992), p. 122.

[5] Susan Schechter, *Women and Male Violence*, p. 5.

[6] Ibid., p. 318.

[7] Ibid.

[8] "Making Rape an Election Issue," in *Transforming a Rape Culture*, p. 216.

[9] "Clarence, William, Iron Mike, Tailhook, Senator Packwood, Spur Posse, Magic...and Us," in *Transforming a Rape Culture*, p. 135.

[10] *Transforming a Rape Culture*, p. 92.

[11] Ibid., p. 93.

[12] Kimmel, "Clarence, William...and Us," p. 125.

[13] See Pat James, Do it Yourself Self-Defense," and Nadia Telsey, "Some Facts on Self-Defense" in *Fight Back, Feminist Resistance to Male Violence*, ed. F. Delacoste and F. Newman (Minneapolis: Cleis Press, 1981).

[14] Nathaniel Altman, *Ahimsa* (Wheaton, IL: Theosophical Publishing House, 1980), p. 5.

[15] Matthew Fox, *A Spirituality Named Compassion* (San Francisco: Harper & Row, 1990 edition).

VI DESPAIR AND EMPOWERMENT

1. Apathy

Signals of distress are everywhere. Feelings of despair are not uncommon or surprising. In many ways, feeling despair is a healthy response to the magnitude of violence increasing in our world. However, ignoring distress caused by violence interferes with healing and social change. A healthy response calls us to reach into every part of our lives, including our despair, in an attempt to bring deeper awareness to the suffering within and around us.

Most individuals and communities resist such reaching, and so cause distress and despair to escalate. We often hide or distance ourselves from feelings of despair. The problem of violence is so big, and we may feel overwhelmed or powerless to effect change. We sometimes make the decision not to face the suffering that violence brings, and become apathetic. Apathy (a Greek word—*apatheia*—meaning non-suffering) is prevalent in many communities.

The cause of apathy is linked to indifference. However, if we look more deeply, we will find the cause of our apathy stems more from the fear we feel surrounding despair than from indifference. Apathy is a defence that prevents one from facing fear. It is a refusal to feel that, unattended, creates numbness and ultimately, non-action.

2. Psychic numbing

Arnold Mindell, in his work with global conflict, finds that the oppressed individual or group suffers not only because of trauma from past abuses but also *because of the present intolerance to his or her suffering.*[1] Why do we have so little tolerance for the pain of an oppressed individual or group?

There are social taboos against expressing despair, because of fear. We are living in an "age of anxiety" and have become "adept at sweeping our anxieties under the rug."[2] Our despair is rarely expressed directly and often is pushed underground. Ongoing suppression of despair about violence creates what many call "psychic numbing."[3] What becomes censored or held back eventually creates a hardening or numbing of the self to the truth of violence. And like anything frozen, our numbness prevents what is vital to life from growing. The self becomes impoverished—a form of poverty that is often manifested through low self-esteem, depression, illness or aggression. Soldiers experience this as shell-shock.

Absenting ourselves from the violence in our lives is socially condoned. The message often given is: don't talk about it, don't feel the pain, and if your grief is too deep we can medicate or institutionalize it. Joanna Macy, a scholar and social activist, teaches through despair work that *the refusal to feel*

> impedes our capacity to process and respond to information. The energy used in pushing down despair is diverted from more creative uses, depleting the resilience and imagination needed for fresh visions and strategies.[4]

We lose strength and knowledge by not attending to the reality of despair in our lives. We may filter out information that is profoundly important to learning how to tolerate and transform suffering.

3. Wound as healer

We have learned from soldiers suffering from shell-shock and sexual abuse survivors suffering rape trauma that the healing resides in the wound. The wound must speak. Our truths, including our despair, must be attended to even when they are terrible. In the exile we often experience when we are made to feel "different" for the oppression we suffer, we are longing for release.

We can find our way through numbness by telling our stories in an atmosphere of trust and openness and by questioning our own collaborative assumptions about violence and nonviolence. We *locate* rather than displace our despair. We question the tolerance of oppression. We find ways of acknowledging the trauma of past abuse and we find ways of being fair witnesses to the suffering in others. Eventually, we need to acknowledge that our despair belongs in our process of nonviolent change. Drawing closer to our despair, we can begin to dissolve the numbness and heal the brokenness in our lives.

THE PROCESS ENCOURAGES US PURPOSELY TO BRING ALL THE NEGATIVITY TO THE SURFACE, TO EXAMINE IT, TO FACE IT IN ITS COMPLEXITY AND DEPTH, AND TO SURRENDER IT, HOLDING NOTHING BACK SO THAT WE MAY DISCOVER NEW INSIGHT, STRENGTH AND WHOLENESS. WE MOVE, IN FACT, THROUGH THE PHASES OF GRIEF, FROM DENIAL THROUGH ANGER, DEPRESSION, DISORIENTATION AND ON INTO A NEW BASIS FOR SOLIDARITY, EMPOWERMENT, HUMOR AND HOPE. FOR AS WE SHARE THESE DEEPER EXPERIENCES WITH EACH OTHER, WE DISCOVER THE HEALING PERSPECTIVE OF THOSE WHO DARE TO HOLD ONTO A VISION TOGETHER.

—*FAMILY VIOLENCE IN A PATRIARCHAL CULTURE MANUAL*

4. Waking up

IT IS HARDER TO LOVE THE WORLD THAN TO DENOUNCE IT, HARDER TO EMBRACE EXISTENCE THAN TO RENOUNCE IT.

—JAMES BROUGHTON

Despair and empowerment work calls us to awaken out of our slumber. Repression of feelings makes us violent and/or passive. Violence deadens our senses. Passivity puts us to sleep. As walking wounded we are often sleep-walking our way through existence, disconnected in ways that deepen despair. Nonviolence, on the other hand, requires wakefulness and connection. It requires we begin with ourselves, the practice of *ahimsa*—dynamic compassion—by bounding back into our bodies with the attentive intention to feel and to listen. Nonviolence asks that we patiently pay attention to what is going on with open eyes and ears and hearts. Our dark nights of the soul have a purpose. Often, it is between despair and self-questioning that insight comes to us and meaning comes full circle.

The power of doing despair work in a community setting is learning we need not be alone with our pain or fear. In community we can discover connections through despair work and empowerment through nonviolence education. We can support each other in our awakening. This depends in part on whether we create relationships based on caring or control. Despair work is caring for rather than controlling our fears.

Waking up also depends on healthy living—learning to take care of ourselves by refusing toxic substances and lifestyles that deaden our life energy and our capacity to be calm and alert. Can we let go of these substances and lifestyles? Can we choose to hear the other without taking control of her/his experience? Can we lean into our own and others' truths mindful of the resistance and open to the journey?

5. Advocates and activists

MORE THAN A THOUSAND USELESS WORDS IS ONE SINGLE WORD OF PEACE.

—UPANISHADS

There are many advocates and activists who are working in the public spheres of society for social justice and nonviolent transformation. The courage demonstrated by many of these workers is often unacknowledged and unnoticed. Much of the work, like parenting, is invisible. The days and months that are devoted to organizing a peaceful demonstration; the networking, consulting and sharing that occurs by mail, phone and travel; the immense pooling of economic, emotional and educational resources are just some examples. Nonviolent advocates and activists have brought and continue to bring living examples of complementarity in which the unity and diversity of humankind move from either/ or paradigms to models of inclusivity and openness. The gift of complementarity in social justice work, as in nonviolent parenting, is one that teaches again and again that in our multi-dimensional facets as humans are extraordinary creative possibilities when we open to our differences and are mindful of our similarities.

Advocacy and activism often grow out of a great faith in local solutions to problems. The goal of keeping participation in social change relevant and responsible to the particular community we live in makes the work meaningful in everyday terms. When the work is closer to home it can help us respond more sincerely to injustice that is not home-based. The global reality of suffering and the possibility of nonviolent solutions become clearer through the networking of nonviolent action across our lives. Advocates and activists around the world have done much to de-institutionalize systems of learning and distribution of resources, particularly loosening control of information.

Reshaping systems and institutions requires unyielding persistence, and if it is to succeed, peaceful intent. Here, *satyagraha* is protected through the goodwill, friendship and strength of allies working together for true equality and peace. This effort, as so many advocates for battered women and abused children have demonstrated, is a form of power-with that walks alongside those in need with the intention to understand and honestly make a difference. Alliance-builders that begin anew each day with imagination and integrity provide great antidotes to crisis. Antidotes that, if we open to them, can benefit all.

WHAT DO YOU SUBSTITUTE FOR HOPE? POSSIBILITIES, POSSIBILITIES... YOU CAN'T PREDICT. JUST MAKE SPACE FOR THEM. THERE ARE SO MANY.
—JOANNA MACY AND JIM DOUGLASS

6. Empowerment and service

All oppressed groups suffer loss of power—the ability to self-determine and exercise basic freedoms. The goal of a dominator is to undermine or destroy the strength of power and liberty residing within a human being. In short, an oppressor seeks to render a person, group or nation powerless through violence and the removal of human rights. To do this, an oppressor participates in acts of dehumanization that, in the circumstances of women, are of catastrophic proportion.

I WANT TO WRITE, BUT MORE THAN THAT, I WANT TO BRING OUT ALL KINDS OF THINGS THAT LIE BURIED IN MY HEART.
—ANNE FRANK

Women across the world share the threat or experience of disempowerment. Violence against women is the most common injustice of human rights.[5] Worldwatch reports make clear this is not random violence.[6] In all instances of violence from rape, battering, genital mutilation, infanticide, cruel neglect, dowry-motivated murders, honor-killings...women are targets of violence because of their gender.

FOR NATIVE PEOPLES, "SOVEREIGNTY" IS NOT WHAT COMES THROUGH "RIGHT TO CONQUEST" (THAT IS, POWER OVER THE OSTENSIBLY WEAKER, OR THE MORE VULNERABLE), BUT RATHER SIGNIFIES EMPOWERMENT THROUGH SELF-REALIZATION, SELF-REPRESENTATION AND SELF-DETERMINATION.
—INÉS HERNÁNDEZ-ÁVILA

Only the oppressed fully understand their oppression; so only the oppressed understand how to dismantle their oppression.[7] Liberation, as a struggle to resist the limitation of freedom to basic human rights, challenges the power of an oppressor. When that power is challenged, the group with that power, if it does not give up its use of power over others, must enforce that power through violence—covertly or overtly.[8] "The experience," Judy Webb explains, "of an oppressee differs from the experience of a loss of previous power by an oppressor."[9] This difference lies in the *conditions* of those giving or receiving power.

We cannot "empower" anyone but we can be for the empowerment of ourselves and others. Empowerment is the result of freedom to choose for oneself practices which increase personal health and social consciousness. To support a process of empowerment is to open to a recovery process of reclaiming dignity, self-determination and the development of ideas that benefit humankind. Empowerment is the ability to grow fully into one's power of truth. It is a power that resides within a human being. We cannot give or receive this kind of truth; it is self-realized and fluid.

The power of truth that seeks to increase lovingkindness in the world is able to give in new ways, which are often realized through service. This is not the kind of giving girls and women have been disempowered by—the martyrdom or manipulation of self, the diminishment of desire or accommodation to that which denies our intelligence, freedom or difference. It is not gratuitous.

EMPOWERMENT IS MUTUAL.
—CHRISTINA BALDWIN

Nor is it the kind of giving often taught to boys and men—to give to others in the spirit of a calculated return, of profit, of gaining control or denying one's own emotional needs.

Empowerment creates the kind of giving that brings mutual benefit, a benefit that generates living process and health, giving and receiving, complementarity and congruence with natural laws of balance and beauty. When we participate in a paradigm of empowerment it is possible to enjoy the movement of life and an abundance of love, a giving that is honest. If we can learn to give without calculation or grandiosity, perhaps then we can invent a new way of existing together where giving is for the sake of growth, happiness and transformation.

Notes

[1] Arnold Mindell, *The Leader As Martial Artist: An Introduction to Deep Democracy* (Harper: San Francisco, 1992), p. 92.

[2] Joanna Macy, *World as Lover, World as Self* (Berkeley, CA: Parallax Press, 1991), p. 15, in reference to Arthur Koestler, *Beyond Reductionism: New Perspectives in the Life Sciences* (London & Co., 1969).

[3] *Psychic numbing* is a term first used by Robert Lifton in his study of Hiroshima survivors.

[4] *World as Lover, World as Self*, pp. 15-16.

[5] *World Watch* (March/April, 1989).

[6] Ibid.

[7] So much more has been said and needs to be said about dismantling oppression. Audre Lorde's work, particularly her essay "The Master's Tools Will Never Dismantle the Master's House," in *Sister Outsider* (New York: Crossing Press, 1984) and Paulo Freire's work, *The Pedagogy of the Oppressed*, (Penguin, 1978) are great teachings.

[8] *War on Women*, a statistical and definitional handout, p.3.

[9] Excerpted with permission from a letter written in August, 1994.

VII ANGER AND ACTION

1. Responding to our anger

A s with our despair, can we stare straight into the face of our anger? Can we declare the trauma of our mental anguish as "the grim reality that the culture at large denies?"[1] And can we allow the strength of our anger to mobilize change without harming others in the process?

Linking anger with nonviolent action requires awareness of patterns of reaction. If we hide our anger from our awareness or act out our anger in destructive ways, we cause more suffering. Anything repressed often returns larger in size, in the same way that compulsion creates addictive habits. A middle path responds to rather than reacts from anger. It explores carefully the reasons for anger and then seeks to address injustice and cruelty without reacting blindly. Nonviolent redress of injustice can take many forms but always depends on a quality of mind and heart that is not trapped in patterns of reaction.

Patterns of reaction can begin when we are very young. Children are generally not hostile until they are mistreated. Anger and hostility is often the first layer of our experience. Underneath is suffering. It is because we are unable to reach the pain in ourselves that we cause pain in others. We repeat the cycle of violence and suffering through unchecked pain and anger.

Most oppressive systems can be linked to distancing, repression and failure to understand one's own mindstates. Charlene Spretnak explains:

> Militarism, political oppression, exploitative economic arrangements, and a range of other aggressive acts have been traced to defensive psychological reactions stemming from deep-seated fear and self-loathing. The perpetrators are dominated by a stream of negative mindstates. They are pathologically ignorant of compassion, lovingkindness, joy in the joy of others, and

OUR TASK OF COURSE, IS TO TRANSMUTE THE ANGER THAT IS AFFLICTION INTO THE ANGER THAT IS DETERMINATION TO BRING ABOUT CHANGE. I THINK, IN FACT, THAT ONE COULD GIVE THAT AS A DEFINITION OF REVOLUTION.
—BARBARA DEMING

equanimity—except in the limited ways allowed by their fear and pain. The ecstatic truth of interbeing escapes them. This is true also of people who exhibit disrespectful, dominating behavior on a smaller scale as well. Ignorance constricts and diminishes them.[2]

Our lives call us to actively work through our experiences in mindful ways. This means bringing attention to the mental torment that directs the habits and outbursts of an abusive, dominating person.

Unexplored anger is dangerous and isolating. When we view anything as separate, as the "other," our anger becomes our enemy rather than an important message needing responsible attention. Typically, we repress our anger or throw it around. Condemning or clinging to our anger causes it to implode or explode. We can destroy ourselves or others with anger if it stays unchecked.

2. Taking tea with the demons

Anger that does not injure requires what Stephen Levine describes as "taking tea with the demons of our holdings."[3] Only merciful exploration of our anger, he says, can liberate our patterns of aversion and blind reaction. This requires we take responsibility for our anger by *relating to* rather than *reacting from* it. This is no easy task yet is essential if we are ever to discover the injury of the world that is contained in our own anger, underneath which there is love that has been refused and which we now refuse ourselves and those around us.

To be responsible for our anger is to bring it within the realm of the voluntary. This is not being angry for being angry. It is seeing anger as a fluid process, as connected to other states and feelings such as fear, pain, frustration, abandonment, self-pity, self-righteousness, aggression, confusion and sadness. It is bringing anger into a voluntary realm open-heartedly rather than making it rigid through an aggressive and closed heart. We can take a moment to breathe and pay attention to our anger as it begins to arise before we decide how to direct it.

If we do, we see that anger is often a response to loss and therefore is related to grief. Taking time to sit quietly with our inner turmoil, we increase the chances for resolute healing and straightforward commitment to undoing injustice. Anger is not the problem. It is the way we relate to it that creates violence. Barbara

AND SHIVER NOT
FROM MEMORY/
OR TERROR/
BUT ANGER THAT
THIS WOUNDED
BODY/ MUST *TAKE
A STAND* AND
CRY OUT AS ONLY
A NEW BORN BABY
CAN CRY—/
I LIVE,
I WILL LIVE
I WILL TO LIVE
IN SPITE
OF HISTORY/
*TO MAKE HISTORY
IN MY VISION
OF PEACE*—
—KIMIKO HAHN

IN THE END,
OUR ONLY
DIFFERENCE IS OUR
UNWILLINGNESS
TO HAVE A
FACE TO FACE
CONFRONTATION
WITH THE ABJECT.
—JULIA KRISTEVA

Deming suggested,

> that if we are willing to confront our most seemingly personal
> angers, in their raw state, and take upon ourselves the task of
> translating this raw anger into the disciplined anger of the search
> for change, we will find ourselves in a position to speak much
> more persuasively...about the need to root out from all anger the
> spirit of murder.[4]

Allowing ourselves the space to respond mindfully creates
room for movement into strength, love and determination. We have
a choice.

3. Speaking out

...MY ANGER...
BOTH A SIGN
OF HEALTH AND
ESSENTIAL TO
OUR LIFE AS AN
ADVOCATE OF
NONVIOLENCE.
IT IS EVIDENCE
OF MY LOVE FOR
LIFE. WITHOUT
THE ANGER I'D
PROBABLY BE SILENT
AS STONE, PASSIVE,
COMPLACENT.

—PAM McALLISTER

Our voices are a powerful tool. For many of us this can mean
learning to say no and speaking, with resolute determination, of
our refusal to accept violence in any part of our lives. We are needed,
women and men, to have conversations with each other at home
and in community in which we look carefully at the forms of power
and privilege that are exercised in our relationships. We are also
needed to contribute to a discourse that is unafraid to openly
criticize the development of authoritarianism out of the
fundamentalism and corruption of the nation's infrastructures—
the economic, political, educational and religious systems of power
affecting this whole planet. More than anything, we are needed to
articulate alternatives that are positive, collaborative and
comprehensive.

OUR SLANDERED
WRATH IS OUR
TRUTH, AND—/
IF WE HONOUR
THIS—/ CAN DEAL
NOT DEATH
BUT HEALING.

—BARBARA DEMING

Speaking out about violence against women and children and
the survival of this planet requires we not deny or subvert anger
that arises from experiences of exploitation. An open, intelligent
discourse understands anger as a natural response to repression
and injury, and uses the strength of nonviolent anger for creative
and powerful change. "We need a renaissance of hope which anger
can bring," write Andrea Juno and V. Vale, "stuck as we are in the
midst of an existential, angst-ridden *culture of cynicism* which has
helped implant a widespread attitude of passivity and submissive
acceptance. (No longer are people habituated to *create*, but to
consume—and desire is escalated to such addictive thresholds that
satisfaction remains forever out of reach.)"[5]

Feminism is inseparable from women's voices. The creative
power demonstrated through social change—when women's
voices are an integral part of policy-making, philosophical

remapping of culture and artistic revision—is transformative. Learning to speak out means learning to communicate our emotions and to release the liberty residing in each creative, legitimate and healthy expression of anger. Liberation of voice is central to any freedom.

In her essay, "The Veils," Louise Edrich examines the necessary ownership of the word "no" in our refusal of violence. She writes:

> To hold the word *no* in my mouth like a gold coin, something valued, something possible. To teach the *no* to our daughters. To value their *no* more than their compliant yes. To celebrate *no*. To hold the word *no* in your fist and refuse to give it up. To support the boy who says *no* to violence, the girl who will not be violated, the woman who says, *no, no, no. I will not*. To love the *no*. To cherish the *no*, which is so often our first word. *No*—the means to transformation.[6]

Young girls can be incapacitated if taught that anger can only be negative and undesirable and never creative or mobilizing. An ethic of "niceness" only maintains the compliance necessary to keep women silent and subservient. What our daughters need is encouragement to find their own voices, to express the full range of their emotions and to be defiant when confronted with abuse.

Can we recognize the differences in women's voices and the centuries of conditioning that have undermined women's power of speech? Breaking the lock off women's speech has unleashed a wealth of leadership and literature that is revolutionizing language, relationship and culture. As we travel further in creative action for nonviolence and emotional growth we are finding there are outlets for discovery and evolution that are moving far beyond the destructive ideology of binary dualism and fixed identity. We are moving into a consciousness that is very much alive in its capacity for expressing the immense beauty, multiplicity and dignity in human experience and expression.

RENUNCIATION IS A PIERCING VIRTUE/ NO IS THE WILDEST WORD CONSIGNED TO LANGUAGE
—*EMILY DICKINSON*

THEIR ANGER, WHICH THEY BEGIN TO ACKNOWLEDGE, WE RECOGNIZE AS OUR ANGER; THE STRENGTH WHICH THEY HAVE DOUBTED, BUT WHICH THAT VERY ANGER HINTS AT, IS OUR STRENGTH TOO.
—*BARBARA DEMING*

4. Men stopping male violence

It is not the victim's responsibility to leave an abusing partner; it is the responsibility of the one abusing to stop the violence and commit to change. The truth, though, is that many women do leave, have left many times or are in the process of trying to leave. Women have left thousands of battering men but still men don't stop beating, raping, stalking, harassing and murdering women. As many activists have said again and again, it is not the responsibility of someone to stop another from abusing, nor is it possible to do so. If we choose to be violent, we will be. If we can imagine nonviolence, then that is possible. It isn't a question of women being strong or healthy or wise enough to leave—they do leave. There are also women who will choose a battering relationship over poverty or exile from their communities. The question is whether men are willing to stop abusing.

A starting point is charging and sentencing those who abuse. This way, the principle that rape and assault are criminal acts and are wrong is upheld in society's eye. Other conditions must also be in place to support men changing. These are conditions in which men directly act to resist violence and promote alternatives to systems that condone power over one another. This includes promoting conditions for women that reduce poverty and improve participation in economic and political decision-making. Expecting a victim of violence to give up basic rights to home and community institutes yet another level of injustice. Whenever this expectation is imposed and the offender is not required to leave or be held accountable for stopping the violence, the victim is held responsible and to some degree, blamed for her circumstances.[7]

Resisting violence is difficult and often an impossible hardship for someone trapped in its cycle. In most abusive relationships, unless there is intervention, the violence will occur more often and will worsen, potentially leading to death. It is widely documented that living in an abusive relationship and coping daily with trauma erodes a victim's capacity for helping herself and her children. What society often calls "craziness" or "helplessness" in a victim are, in reality, immense survival mechanisms. The enormous expectation put on abused women to leave their homes can severely compound the confusion around where the responsibility for the violence truly lies. Many women "see themselves as responsible both for what happens to them and for the caretaking of men."[8]

All over the world crimes of violence against women and children are ignored and allowed. It is a rare event to see men in their communities taking an active stance against the violence that their peers are perpetrating. Why are fathers and brothers of this world not rising up against the male violence that harms so many daughters and sisters? How long must women and girls live in societies that seriously undermine and resist knowledge of

BECAUSE EVERYTHING WE DO AND EVERYTHING WE ARE IS IN JEOPARDY, AND BECAUSE THE PERIL IS IMMEDIATE AND UNREMITTING, EVERY PERSON IS THE RIGHT PERSON TO ACT AND EVERY MOMENT IS THE RIGHT MOMENT TO BEGIN.

—JONATHAN SCHELL

women's pain?[9] Helga Jacobson and Naida Hyde, in their article on violence against women and children in British Columbia, give clear examples of how our courts and universities still refuse to take seriously the continuation of abuse of women and children. These women, along with numerous others around the world, state unequivocally that *men who are seen as being highly educated and who have positions of power in medicine, law, education, and politics need to take the responsibility to re-educate themselves and their brothers to cease their violence against women and children. Men must start naming male violence against women and lobby for real political and financial support to end the sexism and misogyny eroding families and culture.*[10]

Pro-feminist men (for which male violence against women is understood as institutionalized by men and caused by social conditions that generally promote, legitimize and minimize its effects) have been the most involved group of men working to stop violence against women. Where there have been no organized activities among pro-feminist men, there has been little resistance by other groups of men to the atrocities faced in women's lives. Particularly, the collective responsibility of men for resisting male violence and for advocating nonviolence is still young and minimal in its development.[11] Often, many men's responses to violence impede individual change and social action by passively looking for "meaning" in abusive behavior rather than actively refusing to repeat crimes of male violence or address their origins.[12] It is common practice nowadays to turn a male offender into a victim and remove the focus of justice from his behavior or the effects on the victim.

Liberation of self and transformation of society are not separate events. As Joanna Macy tells us, "the world itself has a role to play in our liberation. Its very pressures, pains and risks can wake us up...."[13] We need to take care, as we engage in healing ourselves and the world, that one is recognized as necessary to the other. If our resistance work is to embody both intelligence and rigor, we need to be clear that what we do not accept and what is in need of protection require social action that is deeply rooted in an attempt at harmlessness and a desire "to come home to our mutual belonging."[14] Our persistence must be relentless in the two hands of nonviolence (refusing to be a victim while reaching out to the suffering in the abuser) and the belief in a way of living that is not doomed to destruction.

IT IS NOT NECESSARY TO CHOOSE A LIFE OF DRAMATIC SACRIFICE: IT IS NECESSARY THAT WE DISCOVER WHAT WE LOVE THAT IS BEYOND OUR OWN CONCERNS, AND LOVE IT ACTIVELY. TO WORK IN THE WORLD LOVINGLY MEANS THAT WE ARE DEFINING WHAT WE WILL BE FOR, RATHER THAN REACTING TO WHAT WE ARE AGAINST.
—CHRISTINA BALDWIN

THERE IS A HEALING DEEPER THAN RESISTANCE.
—ROSALINDA RAMIREZ

5. Relentless persistence

Despite the toll on women, many are increasingly finding the courage to refuse to accept violence in their lives, sometimes after days, months, or decades of abuse, others after the first sign. Leaving behind dangerous situations of abuse in which they are made to feel inferior, women are finding another way—a reinvention of self that is life-affirming, strong in its interest in justice and uncompromising in its pursuit of self-determination. The essentialist paradigm of women as passive and uninventive has too long undermined women's capacity to refuse deadening and degrading relationships. By fully voicing women's reality and breaking out from under systems of domination and oppression, there is a powerful shift occurring all over the globe in which women are determining their lives with dignity and peace. The dominator paradigm is collapsing as women and men everywhere reconceptualize models of personal and political health.

Prevention of violence against women and children happens when it is accepted as the responsibility of citizens and legislators alike to change the conditions that perpetuate violence. Shelters are not preventative in the long run; not until transition houses across the nation are empty and our homes are safe will we know that we are truly successful in stopping violence and assisting recovery. Cultural beliefs, limited resources and lack of immediate response to hold the abuser accountable all contribute to keeping a victim trapped in an abusive relationship. The minimizing and rationalizing of male violence continues in an alarming fashion. The denial is both private and public and needs unceasingly to be addressed.

WE ARE A PEOPLE THAT FOLLOW AFTER THOSE THINGS THAT MAKE FOR PEACE, LOVE AND UNITY; IT IS OUR DESIRE THAT OTHERS' FEET MAY WALK THE SAME, AND WE DO DENY AND BEAR TESTIMONY AGAINST ALL STRIFE AND WARS AND CONTENTIONS.

—*Quaker Peace Testimony*

In Brazil, *firmeza permanente,* translated as "relentless persistence," has been used to describe nonviolent resistance. This definition of nonviolence emphasizes the constructive nature of struggles against violence, struggles that embody enduring courage. Successfully mobilizing mass numbers of people against violence against women and children is a universal movement that requires a form of "people power" not yet seen in global efforts. Yet the "people power" demonstrated through individuals and organizations working at the grassroots has been unfailing in the work of calling attention to the suffering of women and the provision of sanctuary to those most at risk.

Women and children are forced to "disappear" in countries

that are extolled for their democracy and justice. Women involved in the global battered women's sanctuary movement have had to hide many children from sexually abusive parents and many women from dangerous men. We live in a time where some of our own sisters are fugitives trying to find safety for themselves and their children, help that is primarily provided by children's rights, feminist and religious organizations.[15] It is time that women's organized resistance to male violence is embraced by more than these groups.

6. Resistance

Generations of women who have organized across the globe have successfully broken the silence surrounding the horrors of abuse in women's and children's lives. Contemporary nonviolent resistance work, which seeks to stop violence against women and children while generating restoration and healing, is all around us. The women and men who are committed to this work are examples of how our lives can begin to reshape oppression into liberty and denial into creativity. These are most often the actions of ordinary people who are expressing deep concern for the health of the human family and this planet.

There are many ways of expressing our concern and taking action. Resisting violence can begin by educating ourselves on the dynamics of oppression and addiction, by listening, talking, studying and actively taking a place in the recovery of dignity and wholeness in our own lives. Resistance to violence against women is also often demonstrated through letter-writing, making timely phone calls, boycotts, theatre, painting, exposés, pickets, demonstrations.... Personal and social action against violence is as diverse and inventive as our imaginations allow.

A glimpse into some current examples of social action work in Western Canada and the U.S. toward ending violence against women demonstrates the diversity of response that is possible.

Forum theatre, which originated with Theatre of the Oppressed, is a powerful example of bridging education, action and healing in communities. Here, the political and social context of people's lives, including that of battered women, is dramatized. As Jack Ross describes it, "Through audience involvement, great flexibility of actors, innovation and improvisation, risky material is shaped and reshaped, until basic and often invisible events

NOW SHE IS RISING/ REMEMBER HER PAIN/ REMEMBER HER LOSSES/ HER SCREAMS LOUD AND VAIN/ REMEMBER HER RICHES/ HER HISTORY SLAIN HOW SHE IS STRIDING/ ALTHOUGH SHE HAD LAIN.
—MAYA ANGELOU

AND IT'S DEEP IN MY HEART, I DO BELIEVE, THAT WE SHALL LIVE IN PEACE SOMEDAY.
—CIVIL RIGHTS MOVEMENT HYMN

between the oppressed and oppressor are held together by audience and actors, as truths to be reckoned with.[16]

In the Puentes group (meaning Bridge), led by Lina de Guevara in Victoria, B.C., the participants are most often Latin American immigrants, and refugees new to Canada who are not trained professionally as actors. Embodying their experiences of oppression, loss and persecution through an interactive process that reaches into self and community, this group workshops their life stories into transformative theatre. Performances invite participation from audiences. They work from "fluid scripts" that flow with a spirit of *firmeza permanente* ("relentless persistence") and a belief in the transformation that is possible when people's lives are aligned with creative process, social action, justice and truth.

Beyond Blame, a program of the Nanaimo Nonviolence Society, includes six-month educational groups for abusive men which hold the participants responsible for stopping the abuse while providing alternatives based on nonviolent traditions from ecological, feminist, First Nations, Gandhian, Buddhist and other secular and sacred traditions. Working with the two hands of nonviolence, the program is developing a response to violence against women and children that combines nonviolent resistance to violence with the recovery of a self who is free of the addict/oppressor and is committed to peaceful living.

Resistance is demonstrated by holding men accountable for violence and sharing models of empowerment that support the dignity and responsibility which are integral to living in respectful relationship to self and others, and the land around us. Here, a non-enemy ethic informs a confrontational and compassionate response which teaches the openness, willingness and honesty that are necessary to begin learning alternatives to abusive behavior.

On Saltspring Island a group of local women, now called Saltspring Women Opposed to Violence and Abuse, organized a two-year strategy for ending violence against women in their community through an interactive and educational process. This community group's resistance began as a vigil for an incident of horrific violence in the community. A group of women met and from there formulated responses, beginning by identifying strengths and weaknesses in their community. They identified and addressed myths about their community as a safe place and formed

IF YOU WANT TO IDENTIFY ME, ASK ME NOT WHERE I LIVE, OR WHAT I LIKE TO EAT, OR HOW I COMB MY HAIR, BUT ASK ME WHAT I AM LIVING FOR, IN DETAIL, AND ASK ME WHAT I THINK IS KEEPING ME FROM LIVING FULLY FOR THE THING I WANT TO LIVE FOR.

—*THOMAS MERTON*

a collective for further research and development.

They have since brought together local performers, artists and writers in a production of art, theatre and dance that brought forward the realities of abused women's lives and visionary alternatives to that abuse. Alongside forms of creative action, a crisis line and advocacy resources for abused women have been planned and put in place. Their goal of increasing community awareness through art and active reaching out to abused women integrates an approach that is wonderfully grounded in using the resources which are close by and expanding on an integrated, community-based response.

In the U.S. a group called Doves, organized by Tova Green, Fran Peavey and Carol Perry, found a way to respond to rape survivors in the former Yugoslavia. After hearing about the many thousands of women who suffered from systematic rape and torture during the war there, Fran Peavey asked herself how she could help. An answer eventually emerged and she asked friends to "make bundles of items containing woman's things, like nice scarves, embroidered pillow slips and handkerchiefs, shampoo, soaps, cosmetics—gifts that might enable the women in Bosnia to feel support and connection."[17]

This simple idea quickly grew into a project that, through the strength of informal networking, brought 8,000 gifts of personal items from women (and a few men) in the U.S. and Australia. Tova, Fran and Carol arranged for shipping and travelling and by summer of 1993 were able to personally distribute 4,000 packets of gifts and messages—"bundles of love"—to Muslim, Croat and Serbian women they visited in refugee camps, medical rehabilitation centres, a hospital for raped women, in streets and homes. They met with grassroots international groups working with refugees, resistance workers laboring against the war, and heard many stories of civilians who were killed from refugees who were wounded and still living the consequences of the war.

They returned home "even more committed to resisting hatred wherever we find it in our selves, in our society, and wondering what we could further do." Their next project, in response to the ideas that were given to them by women they met, is to bring another gift, "a human gift," in the form of women performing artists from the U.S., to the refugees and to those working against the war in all three areas: Bosnia, Croatia and Serbia. Describing

THEIR ANGER, WHICH THEY BEGIN TO ACKNOWLEDGE, WE RECOGNIZE AS OUR ANGER; THE STRENGTH WHICH THEY HAVE DOUBTED, BUT WHICH THAT VERY ANGER HINTS AT, IS OUR STRENGTH TOO.
—*Barbara Deming*

WHY DO THEY SHUT ME OUT OF HEAVEN? DID I SING TOO LOUDLY?
—*Emily Dickinson*

this next stage of the Doves project, they tell us: "We want to bring a little relief and creative moments to these women. We are calling this tour "Honoring Loss: Celebrating Life."[18] The birth of this social change project is expanding with every step.

Notes

[1] Charlene Spretnak, *States of Grace* (San Francisco: Harper, 1991), p. 49.

[2] Ibid., p. 46.

[3] Stephen Levine, *Healing into Life and Death* (New York: Doubleday, 1986), p. 228.

[4] *We Are All Part of One Another: A Barbara Deming Reader*, ed. Jane Meyerding (Philadelphia & Gabriola Island: New Society Publishers, 1984), p. 217.

[5] Angry Women, *Re/search* #13 (1991), p. 5.

[6] *Transforming a Rape Culture*, ed. Buchwald, Fletcher and Roth (Minneapolis: Milkweed Editions, 1994), p. 338.

[7] See Anne Jones, *Next Time, She'll Be Dead: Battering and How to Stop It* (Boston: Beacon Press, 1994) for case studies.

[8] Helga E. Jacobson and Naida D. Hyde, "Still Kissing the Rod: Women and Violence in British Columbia," in *British Columbia Reconsidered: Essays on Women*, ed. G. Creese and V. Strong-Boag (Press Gang, 1992), p. 222.

[9] Ibid., p. 223-224.

[10] Ibid., p. 227.

[11] See Ron Thorne-Finch, *Ending the Silence: The Origins and Treatment of Male Violence* for a comprehensive overview of responses among men, including critiques of various groups within the men's movement.

[12] See "I Just Raped my Wife! What Are You Going to Do About It Pastor?: The Church and Sexual Violence," in *Transforming a Rape Culture*, p. 77 for discourse on traditional theological formulations of inappropriate responses to victims of violence and violators.

[13] *World As Lover, World As Self* (Berkeley, CA: Parallax Press, 1991), p. 8.

[14] Ibid., p. 14.

[15] See Pam McAllister, *This River of Courage: Generations of Women's Resistance and Action* (Philadelphia & Gabriola Island: New Society Publishers, 1991), p. 137.

[16] *Nonviolence For Elfin Spirits* (Argenta, B.C.: Argenta Friends Press, 1992), p. 89.

[17] Tova Green, "Defying the Rape Camps—Bundles of Love: Birth of a Social Change Project," *Turning Wheel*, Fall 1993, p. 20.

[18] From the Doves information letter dated March, 1994.

VIII   SELF AND OTHER

1. Fear of the other

We are at war with ourselves and therefore we are at war with one another.[1] It is fear of the "other" or the difference within and outside ourselves that creates the estrangement necessary for violence to occur. Differences that are marked irreconcilable by history, law and cultural patterns create belief systems based on supremacy. Supremacy is the belief in the right to dominance over another group, race, gender or class and it causes racism, sexism, elitism, fascism, heterosexism and ageism. Centuries of "old blueprints of expectation and responses—old structures of oppression,"[2] based on a belief of supremacy, have replaced the practice of welcoming difference as a creative life force to be cherished and respected. As much as we have come to hate others who are different from us, we have begun to disassociate from and even hate aspects of ourselves.

Both victims and perpetrators of violence suffer from fear and hatred. If responses to violence against women and children are reflective of strategies that aim for persecution rather than healing, then systematic demoralization of individuals will continue. Traditional nonviolence theory teaches an opposition to tyrannical systems, often through non-co-operation, without initiating a new cycle of violence and oppression.

2. Distinction and division

The divisions experienced socially, originate within. Internal warfare is recognizable within ourselves through hierarchical dichotomies that split the mind from heart, soul from body, intellect from emotion, and self from other. This separation continues outside of ourselves, witnessed in the conflict between groups that are violently polarized on issues of environment, gender, race, religion and class. All these splits create a fragmented society and

86

remove us from our wholeness. Inevitably, such division distances us from each other and our undeniable interconnectedness.

Wherever a division causes feelings and systems of superiority to dominate, an enemy is created. A culture of violence and secrecy is reinforced through distinctions and divisions of assumed superiority, a superiority we often see enacted in our own families and governments. Since such distinctions persist in this world, we are all affected to one degree or another. In her far-reaching essay "Personal Disarmament: Negotiating with the Inner Government," Deena Metzger describes her own journey of discovering such distinctions and opening to another way:

> I didn't realize how thoroughly I was living the way women have been living in Western culture, thrice colonized, so to speak: first, by living under actual foreign (patriarchal) rule in the world; second, by living under foreign rule within themselves; and third, by being given the task of socializing children according to the dictates of this foreign domination. It has long ago seemed to me that the forms women create reveal co-operative, noncompetitive, nonhierarchical, and intimate patterns that incline toward trust, interrelationship, and peacemaking; but women are socialized and then socialize others into paranoia, conflict and war. I didn't realize that I was living this way and that, in fact, it was not only the way of women, but also of men. We are all living this way.
>
> So even the distinctions between women and men fell away from me. Because the inner world is an unconscious introjection of the outer world, it cannot be selective about the forms that influence it; there is no filter to keep out one system while absorbing another. Each of us breathes in all the tyrannies and dictatorships, all the enslavements and torture. China, Africa, Latin America, the United States, the Soviet Union, Europe, Asia, the Middle East—all come to us democratically in one breath. We are each other. Even as we try to run from each other, try to destroy each other, we are each other.[3]

The continuum of violence that Metzger describes does not allow for any one observable point that we can determine with certainty where an action dominates another. We are all challenged to individually and collectively develop moral sensitivity to what constitutes an oppressive act in each situation we are in. These tasks address each of us in our struggle to remain connected to our own and others' lives. And this entails an ongoing and dynamic effort of nonviolence that seeks to transform division.

I THINK THAT EVERY PERSON SHOULD LOOK AND SEE THAT HE IS HIS OWN COUNTRY, HIS FLESH AND BONES ARE HIS NATION. BY ADAPTING AND CONTRIBUTING THE VALUE OF HIS COUNTRY TO THE PLACE WHERE HE LIVES, HE CAN GET BACK THE BEAUTIFUL THINGS. THAT WAY PEOPLE CAN BE HAPPY AND THEY CAN ALSO CONTRIBUTE TO THE RICHNESS OF THE COUNTRY WHERE THEY LIVE.
—THICH NHAT HAHN

THERE HAS BEEN ONLY ONE WOMAN AND ONLY ONE MAN ON THE MOTHERPLANET, BUT EACH HAS BILLIONS OF FACES.
—JAMIE SAMS

3. Nonviolence as a direction

Social response to violence often draws a strong line between violence and nonviolence. In reality however, and from a global perspective of violence, it is not so easy to draw sides. Thich Nhat Hahn, a Buddhist monk and nonviolence activist exiled from his native homeland Vietnam, says:

> People tend to think of nonviolence more as a technique of action, than a source of strength. There is much focus on the distinction between nonviolence and violence, between nonviolent people and violent people. One can never be sure that one is completely on the side of nonviolence or that the other person is completely on the side of violence. Nonviolence is a direction, not a separating line. It has no boundaries.[4]

Acceptance of self and other depends on this strength. It is the central force behind loving life. It springs from the realization that we are all related and are all eventually weakened by violence.

The concept of enemy is misleading and dangerous to all life on Earth. Only a non-enemy approach to living can stop the destructive roller coaster we are all on. This begins with loving attention to that which we find fearful in ourselves—be it feelings of shame, anger, compulsion or confusion—and the reclamation of a healthy sense of self. The journey home, where self and other can live together despite turbulent difference, is one where "compassion is retrieved from its lonely exile"[5] and used to heal self-hatred. Home becomes a safe place where we can begin to unearth our inner governments for what they are, and open to the fear and lack of knowledge of how to govern ourselves. Can we learn to bring the compassion of harmless love to the monsters we carry inside, which, unattended, are harmfully unleashed everywhere in our daily life?

We are all wounded and wanting. So it begins with ourselves— endlessly crossing over to new territory within; beginning to understand the wounding, fragmentation and confusion; unlearning common patterns of socialization and defendedness which create more suffering. Our brokenness depends on a recovery of self in which practices of healing are based on a search for wholeness and a dissolution of compartments. It is a journey of constant investigation into the fullness of a life that is wide awake and conscious of the creative possibilities of the relationship to oneself and others, free of division.

WHEN ONE IS INJURED, WE ARE ALL INJURED.
—SLOGAN FOR INDUSTRIAL WORKERS OF THE WORLD

4. The complicated truth

Nonviolence theory tells us that our real opponent is not the offender; it is the system that creates the offender and arms him or her with the authority to oppress. The "complicated truth" Deming addresses is the recognition of the oppressed in the oppressor:

> ...if the complicated truth is that many of the oppressed are also oppressors and many of the oppressors are also oppressed, nonviolent confrontation is the only form of confrontation that allows us to respond realistically to such complexity. In this kind of struggle we address ourselves always both to that which we refuse to accept from others and to that which we can respect in them, have in common with them—however much or little that may be.[6]

This, Erik Erikson saw as the struggle to accept "ambivalence in our life." *If, in order to fathom the truth, we must hold on to the potential of love in all hate,* he wrote, *so must we become aware of the hate which is in all love.*[7] Deming urges us to study the complicated truth and ambivalence which exists in each of us. Deming writes:

OUR OWN PULSE BEATS IN EVERY STRANGER'S THROAT.
—BARBARA DEMING

> Only if we accept the presence of ambivalence in the most loving of encounters does truth become what Gandhi means by it—that which supports evolving human nature in the midst of antagonism, because these antagonisms call for conscious insight rather than moralistic repression.[8]

If we divide ourselves through rejection or repression of the commonality linking us all, we further the possibility for violence. Our commonalities point to possibilities of healing within victim and tyrant—the transformation that occurs where there is ongoing healing of our defensiveness or inner warfare. By refusing to divide our hearts against another, we decrease the distance between winners and losers. The chance for all sides to win, then, is increased.

We can reject a person's violent behavior or a system's oppressive law while preserving the dignity in all. As Barbara Deming wrote in "Revolution and Equilibrium,"

> we can put more pressure on the antagonist for whom we show human concern. It is precisely solicitude for his person in combination with a stubborn interference with his actions that can give us a very special degree of control (precisely in our acting both with love, if you will—in the sense that we respect his human rights—and truthfulness, in the sense that we act out fully our

objections to his violating our rights). We put upon him two pressures—the pressure of our defiance of him and the pressure of our respect for his life.[9]

Nonviolent action against assault of women is active self-assertion of this defiance and a genuine concern for the person being defied. Again, as Deming so clearly outlined:

> To resort to power one need not be violent, and to speak to conscience one need not be meek. The most effective action *both* resorts to power *and* engages conscience.[10]

5. Codependence

In healthy relationships we are responsible for ourselves and support our family and friends in becoming responsible for themselves. To be self-responsible we need to be free of addictions to power and prestige, unhealthy relationship patterns, material possessions and toxic substances like alcohol and drugs. Addiction intensifies denial, disconnection and disease. It is difficult to feel good about ourselves when we are full of toxins from unhealthy eating and drinking or lack of rest. When we are too busy to pay attention to the cause and effect of intention and action, we often suffer or cause others to suffer. Our self-worth and responsibility depends on loving care of ourselves—our minds and hearts, souls and bodies. Loving care includes finding ways of responding nonviolently to the places of suffering, growth and basic needs in our own lives.

When our self-worth is small it is not easy to practice self-respect. Without self-respect, important limits and boundaries are ignored and sometimes damaged. Although our intention may be one of helpfulness, without self-responsibility our helpfulness is often initiated from a place of fear and insecurity. We take responsibility for others though not for ourselves. Dependence results when this happens and we are no longer helpful to ourselves or to each other. Twelve-step recovery programs call this codependence. When we are codependent we protect and hide each other from important life lessons. We depend on the other to help us weave webs of delusion. Instead of "facing the music" we escape from the realities of our lives and expect others to take care of things.

Mature relationships are interdependent rather than dependent. Nothing is taken for granted. Instead, gratitude and autonomy bring balance and a daily sharing that invites harmony and growth. Differences are honored as well as the qualities that bind people together. Real respect develops when we support the growth in the other without taking control of it and keep our attention on our own responsibilities.

6. Interdependence

As Fran Peavey tells us, "Whatever we face, we face it together."[11] The work of learning to live and work together on this planet is work in which we grow to see the unalterable fact of our interconnectedness. Our communities can respond in ways that encourage understanding of the crises of self, society and environment as inseparable, and in the inseparability of our lives come to an acceptance of the commonality of and responsibility for our condition. "The experience of interconnectedness," Joan Halifax writes, "however one might come to discover it, changes how we perceive the world, and thereby all our relations with the phenomenal world become an expression of an extended self, a self with no boundaries."[12]

This place of no boundary/border resides in our hearts. It is the heart common to each of us that has come to see the suffering in the world as all our suffering, and the transformation possible when our relatedness is seen as nothing less than sacred. In this heart there is no separation or superiority. Domination of self over other is impossible because we genuinely identify with all beings and the mutuality of our relatedness, which is dependent on harmlessness. When we are aware of the fragility of our relatedness we look for ways to strengthen rather than destroy it.

If we look deeply we can see that our differences are endless but each one is like a link on a long necklace that is worn around the neck of this common body—Earth, home to all of us. This necklace is the continuous connectedness between each of us. When our hearts open to this interconnectedness we can see each other not as enemies but as dazzling jewels who are co-responsible for the strength and beauty of the larger creation of which we are all a part. Only through loving relationship can our links endure. Our dependency, then, is not one of attachment and compulsion but an identification with all beings in a spirit of mutual participation that is non-dual, truly helpful, and generous.

OUT BEYOND IDEAS OF WRONGDOING AND RIGHTDOING,/ THERE IS A FIELD. I'LL MEET YOU THERE.

WHEN THE SOUL LIES DOWN IN THAT GRASS/ THE WORLD IS TOO FULL TO TALK ABOUT IT./ IDEAS, LANGUAGE, EVEN THE PHRASE EACH OTHER/ DOESN'T MAKE SENSE.

—RUMI

91

Notes

[1] Ananda Coomaraswamy, *Am I My Brother's Keeper?* (New York: Ayer Publishers, 1947), p. 67.

[2] Audre Lorde, *Sister Outsider* (New York: The Cross Press Feminist Series, 1984), p. 115.

[3] Deena Metzger, "Personal Disarmament: Negotiating with the Inner Government," in *ReVision* 12:4 (Spring 1990), p. 8.

[4] Interview in Catherine Ingram, *In The Footsteps of Gandhi: Conversations with Spiritual Social Activists* (Berkeley, CA: Parallax Press, 1990), p. 87.

[5] Matthew Fox, *A Spirituality Named Compassion* (New York: Harper & Row, 1990), p. xi.

[6] Barbara Deming, *We Are All Part of One Another*, ed. Jane Meyerding (Philadelphia & Gabriola Island: New Society Publishers, 1984), p. 289.

[7] Ibid., p. 211.

[8] Ibid.

[9] Ibid., p. 177.

[10] Ibid., p. 175.

[11] Fran Peavey, *By Life's Grace: Musings on the Essence of Social Change* (Philadelphia & Gabriola Island: New Society Publishers, 1994), p. 161.

[12] Joan Halifax, *The Fruitful Darkness: Reconnecting with the Body of the Earth* (San Francisco: Harper, 1993), p. 138.

IX   DEFENCE AND DISARMAMENT

1. Life as a battlefield

More than ever we are challenged to explore the spiritual as well as the political implications of our fear of each other. Even within our efforts to be nonviolent there can be violence if we assume we know the reality of another person and project those assumptions. Any ideology can become another tyranny when the identification with it becomes static and closed to questioning. Our lives can become trapped in a battlefield of right and wrong.

Our inner and outer laws are not static, despite our will to control and our desire for permanency. Borders between countries are changing rapidly. Fear of military invasion is constant in many countries. In relationships there is also fear, the fear of losing what is secure and what brings new meaning.

We frequently strike out in defence when change threatens the boundaries that define a relationship. We often are threatened by difference and oppose the freedom in another. Our relationships can become battlefields in which our fear is commonly acted out through powerful scenes of control and abuse. We cease being friends and become opponents; once lovers, we become enemies. The differences that once were inspiring become hated.

> INSTEAD OF A STAGE SET FOR OUR MORAL BATTLES OR A PRISON TO ESCAPE, THE WORLD IS BEHELD AS A MOST GRATIFYING AND INTIMATE PARTNER.
> —JOANNA MACY

2. We must all share the crime

There are those of us who do not lay down arms easily. The tragic destructive training most men and women have received denies relationships based on tenderness, openness, interdependence and mutual dignity. Aggressive cultures teach that vulnerability is a weakness and when this vulnerability, which we all possess, becomes a target for violation and ridicule, we often attempt to stay inviolable by developing armor, rigidity and defences.

The tenderness possible in every man and woman is viewed, in patriarchal systems, as something female rather than as a

> IF WE DO NOT ARM OURSELVES WE HAVE PEACE. IF WE ARM OURSELVES, WE HAVE WAR.
> —BERTOLD BRECHT

universal strength that can bring the most difficult conflicts into resolution. Our dominant political systems define strength as the capacity to remain invulnerable and armed. This is a politic that refuses the strength of love, responsibility and generosity, and instead offers protection through systems of opposition and persecution. In this paradigm, protection is either a delusionary or a militaristic employment of power, and it fails in the long run—as in the example of state protection of women from rape, or defence measures in another country at the cost of great civilian loss.

It is an immense abyss, this nation-state of war we carry within and project outward. There are minority supremacist governments within each of us, and they painfully need dismantling.[1] Through complicity or control, we have all created the monster of defence, which penetrates all of our global and personal relationships. *We must all share the crime* for deep healing to take place. In *Women On War: Essential Voices for the Nuclear Age* the editors include Marguerite Duras' stark words:

> ...The whole world looks at the mountain, the mass of death dealt by God's creature to his fellow.... If Nazi crime is not seen in world terms, if it isn't understood collectively, then that man in the concentration camp at Belsen who died alone but with the same collective soul and class awareness that made him undo a bolt on the railroad one night somewhere in Europe, without a leader, without a uniform, without a witness, has been betrayed. If you give a German and not a collective interpretation to the Nazi horror, you reduce the man in Belsen to regional dimensions. The only possible answer to this crime is to turn it into a crime committed by everyone. To share it. Just like the idea of equality and fraternity. In order to bear it, to tolerate the idea of it, we must share the crime.[2]

Is this why fascism is rising again? Will violence against women and children ever end without all of us attending to what gives rise to the mercilessness and ignorance that is at the root of all violence, and also to the courage and determination that is at the heart of nonviolence and a non-enemy approach?

We are all responsible for finding ways of deconstructing the enemy camps, inside and around us. It remains an immense challenge to dissolve the enemy mentality and defence structures we wage against ourselves and others, yet it appears to be the only way forward if we wish our children to inherit more than the ruins of closed hearts.

THERE NEVER WAS A WAR THAT WAS NOT INWARD; I MUST FIGHT TILL I HAVE CONQUERED IN MYSELF WHAT CAUSES WAR.

—MARIANNE MOORE

3. Redefining protection

Are we aware of how our psychological defences can manifest and become physical systems of control and violation? We need not only deconstruct the nuclear bombs planted in the earth; we also need to deconstruct the bombs planted in our psyches—the attitudes and strategies of a defence-consciousness based on tyrannical dynamics, which control our inner as well as our outer conditions. There is a defendedness that betrays the vulnerability common to all humans. It is a defendedness that is militaristic in nature and causes us to harden our hearts to our vulnerability rather than be open to change.

NONVIOLENCE ALSO MEANS THAT MEN ARE RECONCILED TO THEMSELVES, WITH THEIR OWN SPECIES, WITH NATURE AND THE COSMOS. IN A DEEPER SENSE, DISARMAMENT MEANS EXPOSING ONE'S VULNERABILITY.
—*PETRA KELLY*

Since vulnerability is a given of being human, we need to know how to care for ourselves and each other when we are vulnerable. We need to redefine protection. It is profoundly important that we not betray our vulnerability. We need to know our personal limits and be unwilling to be coercively pushed past those limits. Without knowledge of the nature and danger of an oppressor, of when and how violations have occurred to self or others, of the impact violence against women has had and continues to have, of the possibility of future attacks, disarmament and nonviolent resistance will be a form of martyrdom that is unprepared for or forgetful of the harsh realities of this tortured world.

Disarmament is a process that requires much thought and commitment, and it would help many of us to consider this process with full recognition of our own experiences of violence. It is difficult and sometimes dangerous to give up the notion of the enemy unless we understand how and when we have been harmed.[3] Disarmament requires specific knowledge of when and how the consciousness of an enemy is reinforced. It requires careful and respectful deconstruction of the walls that may once have served as protection. Acknowledging the dangers and defences, around and within, with undivided mindfulness and mercy, we can stop living the war. Global disarmament requires each one of us to first, stop the war within. It is this *healthy impulse to turn toward an undivided self* that is in need of protection.

THERE IS A SECRET PERSON UNDAMAGED IN EVERY PERSON.
—*PAUL SHEPARD*

4. A daily questioning, observing, letting go

At what point do we decide to accept the possibility of peace within our hearts? At what point do we decide to stop the war, to disarm the inner weaponry that keeps us separated in a self-administered exile from our own pain and the pain of others, and the healing of that pain? Disarmament is not ever the result of weakness; it is a process of unlayering the deep courage and tenacious wisdom of the heart. It is the steadiness of a self engaged in daily questioning, observing and letting go of defences. This takes tremendous compassion, embracing rather than opposing what we find in ourselves. It asks that we bring gentleness rather than hardness to the feelings and experiences trapped in our hearts, minds and bodies.

While undertaking the process of transforming the dictatorship that ruled her interior self, Metzger wrote:

BUT NO MATTER
WHETHER MY
PROBINGS MADE
ME HAPPIER OR
SADDER, I KEPT ON
PROBING TO KNOW.
—ZORA NEALE
HURSTON

I could not be a democrat in the world or promote democracy while I was a tyrant within. I had tried it. It looked good in terms of papers and deeds, but I had to admit that my efforts were fundamentally ineffective. Each day of my life, I had unwittingly reinforced and reseeded the world with what threatened it, myself, and everyone I knew: tyranny, slavery, militarism. I couldn't hope to accomplish change in the outside world until I changed the inner one.[4]

Metzger entered the enemy camps (the aspects of life and death she feared most) at a time when, as it has been or will be for most of us, "There was no choice; my country—that is, my life—was at stake."[5] In this crisis of conscience her despair gradually gave way to the daily task of instituting an internal government of peace, an institution that we form not by an aggressive demand to become something different but by offering to teach ourselves, daily, gently and protectively, the practices of peace.

5. Crossing the line

A closed view of the dualities (us/them, violent/nonviolent, victim/perpetrator) dictates responses to problems of violence that prevent alliance-building. Those who "cross the line" by refusing to adopt an enemy mentality are often severely ostracized and ruthlessly judged as dangerous. Examples of such far-reaching social justice are sometimes met with murder, as in the case of Martin Luther King Jr., Jesus and the five Maronel nuns working in El Salvador, all of whom opposed injustice while holding the enemy as "beloved." Each was part of a wider resistance against hatred that continued long after their deaths.

Divisionary practices are often a contemporary tool used to alienate rather than respect distinction, and these practices to this point have not prevented war. For many social activists, the line separating victim from violator is not static and is always capable of transformation. Instead of going behind walls of defence, can we cross the social line of moral authority with its use of power over others and look for an alternative? Perhaps one more circular and inclusive in its approach? Paul Kivel, in his work with assaultive men, reminds us of the potential of *power with*:

> It is the power we gain when we come together *with* other people to make change in our lives—when we recognize that we are a community. The system of power we live under breaks down when we reject the cycle of violence and build alliances with one another. We gain strength and power by overcoming the isolation, crossing the boundaries up and down the chart. The hardest alliances to build are across lines of power. We have been hurt directly by people who hold power over us, and it is hard to trust them. It is also hard for them to change.... When these alliances are built, they are very powerful, they contradict the entire system and set of internalized beliefs upon which it rests. They break the cycle of violence.[6]

We can refuse to be divided. We have institutionalized disconnection from ourselves and each other to the point of death. What alternative is left but to move forward in a resistance to violence that is guided by caring for the human family as a whole?

A basic truth that nonviolent activism often requires is putting your body on the line: not turning away from possibility. There are people living privately behind barriers, never touching or creating outside their private worlds. There is emptiness in many people in our society. Overcoming our own resistance to change is essential. *How could you put your life on the line like that?* someone asked Molly Rush, the Pittsburgh grandmother jailed for civil disobedience at a nuclear weapons plant. *Our lives are already on that line,* she said. *My choice was only to set some terms on that.* There is meaning in nonviolent resistance and courage in the decision to include both the violent and nonviolent citizens when we try to change.

AS THE ARMORING MELTS, WE EXPERIENCE OUR VASTNESS.
—STEPHEN LEVINE

YOU MAKE TYRANNY HELPLESS BY REFUSING CO-OPERATION WITH IT.
—GENE SHARP

6. The will to become many hearts

Love, as a precious resource, has for so long been viewed as scarce rather than abundant. Nonviolent acts of resistance and freedom can come from subverting the patriarchal context of love. By refusing to create sides, which apply a rank of superiority to one side or the other, we can allow for reconciliation, which instead applies an attitude of respect for change. We can look to stop the increasing occurrence of violence in ways that do not further hatred and division. These are ways that approach the suffering of all involved and build strength by bridging alliances between movements for justice and peace. Doing so, we have safer opportunities for reaching out to those we fear. As Thich Nhat Hahn tells us, we want

WHEN WE REALIZE THE UNIVERSAL SELF IS IN US, WHEN AND WHAT MAY ANYBODY FEAR AND WORSHIP?

—UPANISHADS

> ...reconciliation...not victory. People completely identify with one side, one ideology. To understand fear and suffering of a citizen of Russia, we have to become one with him or her. To do so is dangerous—we will be suspected on both sides.

> Reconciliation, to understand both sides, is to go to one side, and describe the suffering being endured by the other side and then go to the other side and describe the suffering being endured by the first side. Doing only that will be a great help for peace.[7]

The states of being which invite nonviolence can be quite obvious or extremely subtle. Paralysis from fear prevents a person from recognizing that place of being which is sometimes experienced as an opening into grace or a conquering of hate. Just laws of human rights are strengthened by recognizing states of grace wherein we can reach through fear and acknowledge another person's dignity while refusing to be violated. It requires that we are guided by the wisdom of an open heart, faith in the possibility of friendship and transformation, and discernment of the timeliness of our action.

In our society, change usually occurs through crisis. Times of spiritual or physical crises are often when most of us consider the reorganization of our life. Faced with death, loss or illness we are also faced with our life and the promise it has offered us. What can be different for us during these times in our lives is how we choose to relate to the aspects of ourselves we find most difficult, hidden or despicable.

IF ONE IS TO DO GOOD IT MUST BE DONE IN THE MINUTE PARTICULARS.

—WILLIAM BLAKE

Leaving behind the usual hatred, rejection and numbness, we can try a new way: we can enter our pain not with the old hardness of defence but with a softness of merciful exploration—and each time our exploration gives rise to panic and helplessness, we can attempt to attend to these reactions until we are ready to continue our journey. We may find what Deena Metzger gradually found, a "peacekeeping force that managed to hold another vision (nonviolence) and to continue the careful process of change."[8]

This takes what Joanna Macy described in *World As Lover, World As Self* as going into it for the long haul. She tells us:

> I don't know where we are going to find the will and stamina to restore our contaminated waters and clearcut forests, our dying inner cities if not in the steadiness of the heart...and the capacity to let go of blame.... When I catch myself looking for a quick fix, or assurances of success, or simply a mood of optimism before doing what needs to be done, I think of Bonghpa Tulku and the many exiled Tibetan Buddhists returned to rebuild villages, monasteries, and communities even while the Chinese government continues its occupation and destruction of Tibet. Don't wait, just do it. A better opportunity might not come along. Place one stone atop another. Don't waste your spirit trying to compute your short-term chances of success, because you are in it for the long haul. And it will be a long haul, with inevitable risks and hardships among us all. So, just keep on, steady and spunky like a Khampa pony crossing the mountains. And keep on keeping on, because in the long run it's perseverance that counts.[9]

SOMETHING WE WERE WITHHOLDING/ MADE US WEAK—/ UNTIL WE LEARNED/ IT WAS OURSELVES WE WERE WITHHOLDING/ FROM THIS LAND OF THE LIVING—/ AND THENCEFORTH FOUND SALVATION IN SURRENDER.

—ROBERT FROST

As we persistently return to our life force, feminists have been telling us for centuries, the process of disarmament unfolds. Personal disarmament surrenders the armor of the heart in an effort to invent another way of existing together. It is "the will to become many hearts" and discovering that what we need to recover already exists.

7. Both spiritual and political

By refusing separateness, personal disarmament becomes an exercise that is both spiritual and political. It is no longer either/or. It is both-and. It is inclusive without destroying difference. It is the mind that is open to the reality of those who are suffering and participates whole-heartedly in the healing of violence.

Doing this we see the universality of our predicament. We are all at a crossroads of structural collapse. Can we begin cross-examining our own patterns of disconnection? Doing so we have a better chance of laying down our arms, the internal weaponry, and seeing the ways in which we have internalized the oppressor. We need to look at the social causes for our condemnation and at our own private acts of complicity.

A GLOBAL AWAKENING CAN ONLY HAPPEN FROM A SPIRITUAL AWAKENING THAT IS OF GLOBAL DIMENSIONS.

—MATTHEW FOX

Personal disarmament is recognizing we are, each one of us, part of a wider web damaged by the politics of separation. With that recognition, we reach beyond the walls of disconnection of self from self and of self from other that every victim and offender must face. *The only way to truly "overcome" an enemy is to help him become other than the enemy. If we cherish liberation it needs to be a liberation that frees both the oppressed and the oppressor.*[10] This is at the heart of nonviolence and disarmament.

Notes

[1] Deena Metzger, "Personal Disarmament: Negotiating the Inner Government," in *ReVision* 12:4 (Spring 1990), p. 4.

[2] Marguerite Duras, "We Must Share The Crime," trans. Barbara Bray in *Women On War*, ed. Daniela Gioseffi (New York: Touchstone, 1988), pp. 103-4.

[3] Metzger, "Personal Disarmament," p. 6.

[4] Ibid., p. 7.

[5] Ibid., p. 3.

[6] Paul Kivel, *Men's Work* (New York: Ballantine, 1992), pp. 85-6.

[7] Thich Nhat Hahn, *Being Peace* (Berkeley, CA: Parallax Press, 1987), pp. 69-70.

[8] "Personal Disarmament," p. 4.

[9] Joanna Macy, *World As Lover, World As Self* (Berkeley, CA: Parallax Press, 1991), p. 178.

[10] Thomas Merton, *Gandhi on Non-Violence* (New York: New Directions, 1964), pp. 14-15.

X NONVIOLENCE IN OUR FAMILIES

1. Families today

In many industrial and post-industrial societies the exclusive male-female dyadic relationship is weakening. As more women become socially and economically autonomous and more men learn to be emotionally engaged in caregiving, a shift is slowly occurring. This shift can allow for new expressions of love and relationships— a consciousness of care, community and co-operation marked by an interdependent and multicultural sense of each other, a sense that can strengthen our abilities to care for the wider human family. Families no longer suffice as only being determined by heterosexual marriages defined by traditional gender divisions of labor, and they no longer suffice as definitions of love that do not broaden beyond the confines of the immediate family of whatever form to include others.[1]

WALK CAREFULLY,
WELL-LOVED ONE,
WALK MINDFULLY,
WELL-LOVED ONE,
WALK FEARLESSLY,
WELL-LOVED ONE,
RETURN WITH US,
RETURN TO US,
BE ALWAYS
COMING HOME.
—URSULA LEGUIN

Healthy family units are any individuals living together out of a basis of love and respect. A family, no matter its form or membership, is destroyed when the mutuality and growth of any of its members is undermined. The 1994 United Nations International Year of the Family proclaimed policies that support the family's right to safety and health in its many diverse forms, and the rights of every individual family member. Not until the needs of all family members, heterosexual and homosexual, young and old, are fully recognized and protected through policies and assistance that build a morality of nonviolence, will the intergenerational and international cycle of violence be stopped. This particularly challenges traditions, religious and cultural, which regulate women to an inferior status in the home, workplace, government and in religion.

We know, beyond any doubt, that all forms of oppression— economic, sexual, political—weaken any family's ability to create and sustain healthy kinship based on peace and partnership.

Families are destroyed daily by dominating structures that impose cruelty, authoritarianism and poverty. The United Nations Declaration of the Rights of the Child is terribly violated. Today, trafficking of children occurs in a number of countries. The physical and economic maltreatment of children violates human rights with a brutality often hidden from public knowledge. Sexual abuse of children has entered the marketplace in all parts of the world where children are used in forms of sexual slavery through the commerce of pornography and prostitution. Children's bodies and souls are colonized through inhuman acts that lead to an increasing number of children becoming runaways—homeless, broken and angry human beings who rarely experience the comforts of belonging to a family in which their caregivers would be incapable of transgressing the basic right to freedom from abuse.

We are called to love all of the children, to find ways of not putting any one of them out of our hearts. Today, there is a harsh movement to stiffen prison sentences for child criminals. These children do not need to be persecuted any more than they already have been before they became violent. They need solid state support and persevering caregivers who have the insight and resources to offer opportunities for the recovery of a dignified self who is not threatened by rejection, illiteracy, poverty, loneliness and danger. They need whole societies devoted to non-exploitative democracy that ensures the liberty of its citizens without any form of violation, including the withholding of basic provisions of shelter and food.

There is also an increasing number of children engaging in violent crime who have caring and responsible parents. These children are clear signs that none are untouchable by the problems of violence, which are entrenched through abusive adult role models in the entertainment business, the marketplace and militaristic governments. Children cannot be expected to protect themselves. We are here to be children's protectors, not their pornographers or persecutors.

Child-rearing has many hindrances and deserves our full attention. It is often difficult, but without our effort of securing healthy homes for our children, their potential for full and dignified lives is hardly possible. Children can be incredible teachers for us. They show us, sometimes painfully so, where we are fearful, judgmental and ignorant. If we pay attention to these difficulties with mercy and welcome our children's lessons with gratitude,

AND I AM THINKING ABOUT MY LITTLE SON, HIS BEAUTIFUL BODY AND HIS HUMAN DECENCY I LOVE HIM WITH A STRENGTH I NEVER KNEW.
—LIBBY SCHEIER

MERCY IS THE OPPOSITE OF JUDGEMENT.
—STEPHEN LEVINE

perhaps then we can create changes in our families and in the communities on which they are dependent if they are to flourish. If we welcome them with this perception we can redefine our caregiving. In his book *A Path With Heart*, Jack Kornfield wrote about child-rearing as in itself, a way of spiritual practice dependent on an endless effort to keep an open heart:

> In many countries the nurturing of wise and healthy children is seen as a spiritual act, and parenting is considered sacred. Children are held constantly, both physically and in the heart of the community, and each child is seen as a...unique contributor to humanity. Our children are our meditation. When children are raised by day care and television, in a society that values money making more than its children, we create generations of discontented, wounded, needy individuals. A key to extending practice into the demanding areas of child-rearing and intimate relationships is the same development of patience or constancy as in following our breaths, bringing our hearts back a thousand times. Nothing of value grows overnight, not our children, nor the capacity of our hearts to love one another.[2]

All our children have gifts. We can work together to illuminate these gifts, to help magnify them for our children so they have a sense of how they belong in this life. Our families cannot be "fixed"; they are needed as places where we can help each other to grow to our full potential. John McKnight speaks of families as places of kinship with mutual functions and responsibilities: "Love that grows out of the basis of people who have loved together, worked together, suffered together." He says "our hopes are that needs in a family can be fixed. We are not 'fixable.' Families are not about 'fixing people' but about helping each person learn and manifest their gift in community."[3]

LOVE IS NOT EASY. ONE DOES NOT FALL IN LOVE BUT GROWS INTO LOVE.
—HAKI R. MADHUBUTI

2. Preparing for the day

Daily ritual is important to create a sense of order and a feeling of belonging. With our children we may have active bedtime rituals— a routine where practices such as cleaning teeth, telling stories, songs and prayer, a last glass of water or hug prepares children for sleep. It helps them to let go of the day and enter peacefully into the night. Bedtime rituals are common. Morning rituals are not. Why do we not also help our children prepare peacefully for their day?

Our children need us to help them enter into the complexity of

TELL ME AND I'LL FORGET. SHOW ME, AND I MAY NOT REMEMBER. INVOLVE ME AND I'LL UNDERSTAND.
—NAVAJO SAYING

living with calm and self-assurance. Creating calmness can begin by taking time in the morning with your children to sit quietly and breathe together. This simple practice teaches children and ourselves how to create the inner space that is necessary for listening and self-awareness. It is a way of consciously connecting to our bodies and the signals they give us. Children who are given time to learn to appreciate these signals are better able to identify how they feel and what they need.

A child is empowered by being able to notice and articulate comfort or discomfort as shown through body feelings. Sitting together for ten minutes with the intention of peacefully observing one's inner life teaches one to connect mind, heart and body. It is a form of active nonviolent practice that benefits both the parent and child. It furthers our children's capacity to "be in their truth" and to communicate this truth.

This process lays a foundation for a child to make the connection between how she/he feels and acts. Much of the basis for division in the world begins with early disassociation from ourselves. Exploring this, Susan Griffin writes:

> There are many ways we have of standing outside ourselves in ignorance. Those who have learned as children to become strangers to themselves do not find this a difficult task. Habit has made it natural not to feel. To ignore the consequences of what one does in the world becomes ordinary. And this tendency is encouraged by a social structure that makes fragments of real events. One is never allowed to see the effects of what one does. But this ignorance is not entirely passive. For some, blindness becomes a kind of refuge, a way of life that is chosen....[4]

A quiet time in the morning with children—a walk, a prayer, ten minutes of silence—teaches children to become familiar with their inner lives and begin the day without a sense of strangeness. Our children need care in the broad sense of belonging. They need to feel they belong to themselves in order to move with confidence and wakefulness into the mystery of how to belong in the wider world.

3. Sense of belonging

The main blessing of family is a sense of belonging. Its main wound is a sense of rejection. We can create in our family structures a sense of belonging or exile: a place that feels and becomes like a prison

WE HAVE TO HELP OUR LOVERS, OUR BROTHERS AND OUR FATHERS TO HEAL. THESE ARE THE SONS OF WOMEN WHO HAVE ENDURED AND SURVIVED.... NOW WE MUST TEACH OUR SONS TO GROW TO BE HONORABLE MEN AND TO END THIS TRANSGENERATIONAL POISON OF WAR AND CULTURAL GENOCIDE BY HELPING THEM REMEMBER WHO THEY ARE.

—CINDI MOON
ALVITRE

or a place that safely nurtures the freedom of each individual member. Families can work together to magnify rather than minimize the uniqueness of each person with whom we share responsibility in our homes. Those of us who are born or given to families who don't know how to nurture the individual gifts of children often experience a sense of exile or alienation.

Many people grow up in families where they felt like aliens. All children are not what their parents exactly planned, for each child is inherently unique. Without active respect for the uniqueness of each child, childhood often becomes a circumnavigation of expectations that do not fit well for the child or parent, which can cause us to banish family members and create "outcasts" in our own homes. As Clarissa Estés writes,

> Pressure to be "adequate," in whatever manner authority defines it, can chase the child away, or underground, or set her to wander for a long time looking for a place of nourishment and peace.
>
> When culture narrowly defines what constitutes success or desirable perfection in anything—looks, height, strength, form, acquisitive power, economics, manliness, womanliness, good children, good behavior, religious belief—there are corresponding dictates and inclinations to measurement in the psyches of all its members. So the issues of the exiled...are usually twofold: inner and personal, and outer and cultural.[5]

The inordinate silence or excessive noise expressed by a rejected child can be an indication that some level of banishment has occurred. In most families we have agitating or disturbing ways of controlling, diminishing and silencing the basic truths of those we live with. We can change this.

Silence often accompanies banishment. Though those we live with may wish to speak truthfully, many are pressured to be silent if their truth does not conform to family rules and expectations. No child or adult can fully accommodate this silence or feeling of inadequacy that comes from impossible expectations and the struggle to speak from one's own place of truth. In order for children to be their own selves and to successfully realize their gifts, they must be sheltered from domination and banishment. Otherwise children grow up with the pain of not ever being fully accepted and possibly living in a world where they feel constantly judged. Thus non-acceptance and judgment are learned, gifts go by unrecognized, and a disempowered self enters the public world.

LIFE CONSISTS IN LEARNING TO LIVE ON ONE'S OWN, SPONTANEOUS, FREEWHEELING: TO DO THIS, ONE MUST RECOGNIZE WHAT IS ONE'S OWN, BE FAMILIAR AND AT HOME WITH ONESELF. THIS MEANS BASICALLY LEARNING WHO ONE IS AND LEARNING WHAT ONE HAS TO OFFER.... THE PURPOSE OF EDUCATION IS TO SHOW A PERSON HOW TO DEFINE HIM/HERSELF AUTHENTICALLY AND SPONTANEOUSLY IN RELATION TO HIS/HER WORLD—NOT TO IMPOSE A PREFABRICATED DEFINITION OF THE WORLD, STILL LESS AN ARBITRARY DEFINITION OF THE INDIVIDUAL HIM/HERSELF.
—THOMAS MERTON

4. Toxic shame

All principles and practices of nonviolence begin in our hearts and our homes. Much violent anger is pure rebellion against past control. Alice Miller, in her studies of the childhoods of Nazi leaders, traced the origins of the catastrophic violence of fascism to violent child-rearing practices.[6] A "poisonous pedagogy" of child-rearing based on violent control, conditional love, and denial of feelings begins the process of numbing, disconnecting and desensitizing in a small child. It also creates the reality in a child's mind that abuse is normal. Our children are often forced into roles of victims and offenders long before they have become adults.

In the vortex of violence is a legacy of shame. Teaching shame passes on misery when that shame is "toxic" or laden with rejection, judgment and projection.[7] Anyone repeatedly taught a sense of shame about who they are, as a child, as a woman, or as a man will eventually lose self-respect. When shamed, we are hurt. Nonviolence combats shame by affirming the life of every individual and the right of each of us to a dignified life. Nonviolent child-rearing practices offer a child loving acceptance based on gentle leading and the expression of joy in their presence in our lives.

Toxic shame ultimately prevents children from experiencing unconditional love and from believing this love exists in themselves. Children need to trust themselves and be able to assert their own nonviolent principles and practices in their lives. In order to prevent violence in our relationships we have to practice peace in our homes and value those we live with.

> So many of the problems we deal with are the direct result of children never feeling loved, never feeling special, never feeling worth anything. So many kids in our society are desperately grasping at straws for attention.... They'll take tenderness even if it's preceded by a beating or sexual advance. We could do much toward reducing violence of all kinds if only, as a society, we would communicate that we value our children and that we value women.[8]

All the issues presented in this book can be shared with children in helpful ways if we make time to listen and find supportive ways of sharing how alternatives to violence can be developed. This begins by fully assuring our children of protection from violence, whenever possible, and of being completely accountable if we fail.

This book emphasizes that the opportunity for healing is never lost when our hearts stay open. Our children need to believe in the possibility of healing.

5. No transformation without recovery

We show our children the potential for transformation by participating in our own recovery. We choose as adults the relationships that lend dignity to ourselves, we learn the value of solitude, of community and of honest reflection. *Anywhere an adult family member is consumed by mindstates of anxiety, resentment, and ill will, the entire family is affected.*[9] We begin our reactive patterns when we are very young and as explored in the chapter on Anger and Action, this shapes our capacity for assertive or aggressive anger.

We can suffer for a lifetime if we do not understand these patterns and replace them. We help ourselves further when we heal the shame of the condemned child we may still carry within from our own abusive childhoods. We can

> eliminate such horrors from the lives of future children, a goal (Alice Miller) believes can only be achieved when each adult stops denying, forgetting, or justifying his or her childhood, and thus stops repeating it out of revenge or unconscious patterning.[10]

WE WORK ON OURSELVES, THEN, IN ORDER TO HELP OTHERS. AND WE HELP OTHERS AS A VEHICLE FOR WORKING ON OURSELVES.
—*RAM DASS*

As Anne Wilson Schaef asserts, *we cannot transform without recovery, and recovery cannot happen without transformation.*[11] The task is bringing self-awareness into our lives and providing opportunities for our children to do the same. We can begin daily by living with honesty. We can love ourselves and children enough not to stay in oppressive environments, and we can refuse to create an environment that denies or degrades the life of another. To live truthfully requires unconditional love—families that are devoted to the freedom of their family members, to the human liberation (not confinement) of love, justice and truth realized by each.

As adults we often trap ourselves in the net of social images at the expense of our own authenticity and peace. We each have to find our own way of reconciling past injury in order to learn discernment and recover respect of self and others. The very best effort usually is one that moves toward knowing oneself and learning to speak one's own truth without violence. When one moves toward this knowledge, one can delight in difference and in listening deeply to oneself and others.

Can we let go of the Hallmark version of family, the mythological romantic picture of perfection? Can we look closely at how families have been used as a place for power and control rather than unconditional love and freedom? So much of family systems in dominator cultures is based on a moralistic fabrication of lies in which the human right to question and to learn to govern oneself lovingly is denied. Our families, more than ever, are needed as sanctuaries.

6. Nonviolent parents and caregivers

There are many non-offending, hard-working parents and caregivers—women and men who are committed to change in their families, who are willing to ensure an effort and environment of nonviolence and equality in their home. "In a just society," Haki R. Madhubuti writes, "one's knowledge and capabilities, that is, what one is actually able to contribute to the world, is more valuable than if the person is male or female."[12] Parents who honor their children's value look carefully at gender stereotyping and provide opportunities for each child's expression in ways unfettered by social constrictions on what constitutes femaleness and maleness—most of which are founded on belief systems of domination and submission. For many, Madhubuti writes, this means

> the liberation of the male psyche from preoccupation with domination, power hunger, control and absolute rightness requires an honest and fair assessment of patriarchal culture. This requires commitment to deep study, combined with a willingness for painful, uncomfortable, and often shocking change.[13]

CHANGING THE WAY WE RAISE OUR CHILDREN IS THE ONLY LONG-TERM PATH TO PEACE AND ARMS CONTROL, AND NEITHER HAS BEEN MORE CRUCIAL.
—GLORIA STEINEM

Can we look carefully at definitions of sex roles and rebuild our caregiving so our boys and girls are given fair and equal opportunity to realize their dreams and capacity for learning how to love?

Numerous parents and caregivers love and live in ways that allow the whole being of their children to develop with respect and safety. In these homes there are elements of sanctuary in which all members of the family can find refuge. Home for families in this respect is a safe and restful place where the souls of children are sheltered from undue harshness. A commitment to the wholeness of another, with patient and gentle care, builds a ground of trust. When this trust springs from a practice of nonviolence then our children's chances of realizing joy is very great.

Nonviolence in our families can be defined in many ways, but in all, the intention is to allow the dignity and worthiness of a child to unfold without harm. For this to happen, a caregiver entrusted with the well-being of a child chooses whenever possible to (1) provide a calm, safe and healthy environment; (2) refuse to resort to any form of harm (physical abuse, emotional shaming, control or neglect); (3) be a role model of patience and problem-solving skills; (4) practice unconditional love wherein we respect and encourage the growth of the dignity and worthiness inherent in each human being and protect this dignity when it is threatened by others; (5) ask for and find appropriate help with our parenting when we need it; (6) take time to honor the gift of our family; and (7) take responsibility for our own recovery process.

LOVE HAS TO BE PUT INTO ACTION AND THAT ACTION IS SERVICE... ALL WORKS OF LOVE ARE WORKS OF PEACE.
—MOTHER TERESA

It is important that we affirm those parents and caregivers who bring this kind of effort in their responsibility to children. These men and women are real gifts, not only as protectors of children but as global citizens. They are each role models and practitioners who, like everyone, experience limitation, despair and loss but who are daily practising mindful relationship with their family based on a real desire for the happiness and self-determination of their loved ones.

We all falter. What makes the difference is standing up again and proceeding with our best effort. Our best efforts are strengthened in supportive environments of other caregivers who are committed to the health of themselves and their families. We need to take time to help and honor each other in these efforts, since so much of caregiving is unseen and uncelebrated.

WHEN THE MIND IS AT PEACE THE WORLD TOO IS AT PEACE.
—LAYMAN P'ANG

Notes

1 See Hazel Henderson's essay, "Toward Holistic Human Relationships."
2 Jack Kornfield, *A Path With Heart* (New York: Bantam, 1993), p. 292.
3 Canadian Broadcasting Corporation interview, Open House, January 23, 1994.
4 Susan Griffin, *A Chorus of Stones: The Private Life of War* (New York: Doubleday, 1992), p. 153.
5 Clarissa Pinkola Estés, *Women Who Run With the Wolves* (New York: Ballantine, 1992), pp. 173-4.

[6] Alice Miller, *For Your Own Good: Hidden Cruelty in Child-rearing and the Roots of Violence* (New York: Ferrar, Straus & Giroux, 1983).

[7] See John Bradshaw, *Healing the Shame That Binds You* (Deerfield Beach: Health Communications, 1988).

[8] *Family Violence in a Patriarchal Culture* (Ottawa: The Church Council on Justice and Corrections, 1988), p. 34.

[9] Charlene Spretnak, *States of Grace* (San Francisco: Harper 1991), p. 34.

[10] Gloria Steinem, *Revolution from Within* (Toronto: Little, Brown & Company, 1992), p. 101.

[11] Anne Wilson Schaef, *Beyond Therapy, Beyond Science* (San Francisco: Harper, 1992), p. 182.

[12] Haki R. Madhubuti, "On Becoming Anti-Rapist," in *Transforming a Rape Culture* (Minneapolis: Milkweed Productions, 1994), p. 177.

[13] Ibid., p. 176.

XI NONVIOLENCE IN OUR COMMUNITIES

1. Domination and dominion

Indigenous languages, rainforests and wildlife are disappearing. Fresh water and clean air are disappearing. Patriarchal culture is real. Defined as "rule of the father" or "right to conquer," patriarchal systems dictate law, destroy nature, and desecrate relationships. Patriarchy is an old order of domination and dominion. *Domination is external power which says, "I dominate you. I'm stronger than you. I'll physically overcome you." Dominion is a whole spiritual and mental posture which says, "I am by the grace of God, superior. I have rights over you."*[1]

Privilege in this society has been based on the ideas of patriarchal domination and dominion. It separates people into majority and minority groups, winners and losers, haves and have-nots, persecutors and persecuted, oppressors and oppressed. Minority groups are repressed based on gender, ethnic, racial, religious, economic and social factors. *Sexism is independent of race, religion, nationality or family.*[2] The oppression of women through male violence is a historical fact that is linked to massive male assault on other men, whole nations and our environment. Patriarchal systems of exploitation and warfare threaten the existence of our planet. Our training to be abusive is severely affected by the military and conquest consciousness that is common to many nation states.

Community work that addresses violence against women must link militarism with the oppression of women. Over 20,000 children are reported to have been born as a result of brutal sexual terrorism in Bosnian rape camps during the current civil war. Catherine MacKinnon reported in New York, August 27, 1993 at the preliminary War Crimes Tribunals that there are real women who are willing to testify about their rapes. There are documented accounts ready to be processed. A great many women are so

FEMINISM, ECOLOGY, ETHNICITY, AND TRANSCENDENTALISM (SPIRITUAL RENEWAL), APPEAR TO BE CONVERGING TOWARD A COMMON GOAL.... THE RECOVERY OF OUR BODIES, OUR HEALTH, OUR SEXUALITY, OUR NATURAL ENVIRONMENT, OUR ARCHAIC TRADITIONS, OUR UNCONSCIOUS MIND, OUR ROOTEDNESS IN THE LAND, OUR SENSE OF COMMUNITY AND CONNECTEDNESS TO ONE ANOTHER.

—*MORRIS BERMAN*

111

destroyed they are unable to come forward, but there are many, many, she says, who can. And there is not a just war tribunal, she reminds us, without witnesses.[3]

There have been wars in other countries where women were targeted in a dehumanizing war strategy that aims at crippling whole groups of people through systematic rape and torture. This military sexuality of terrorism carries over into North American culture. Most 18-year-old men have watched 32,000 murders, seen 12 acts of violence an hour on television. Men are more willing to inflict sex-related violence after viewing violent pornographic film.[4] How are we to respond?

2. We are all part of one another

We cannot, if we want transformation in our communities and world, stand outside and fail to be witnesses to all sides of the story.

> The outside world looking in...judges, diagnoses and treats one side or the other in the conflict as subhuman. A group or country in revolution is punished and diagnosed by the rest of the world in the same way that doctors, family members and colleagues act toward someone going through a psychotic episode.
>
> The aloof and superior outside world is often as unconscious about its position as the members of the battle are about theirs. All are possessed by their own states. The outside world fails to see its position as a role in the conflict. Thus, there are no local battles. Every local battle is a world battle in which everyone is a part.[5]

THE ENTIRE
UNIVERSE IS YOUR
COMPLETE BODY.
—CH'AN-SHA

This is also true for violent crimes in our communities. An injury to one is an injury to all. This is another way of saying what St. Paul said some 2,000 years ago. *We are all members of one another, and when the health of one member suffers, the health of the whole body is lowered.*

This century is unique in the magnitude of suffering inflicted by human beings on other human beings. Personal recovery and planetary transformation require that we look into ourselves and our communities, root out the varied forms of cultural and institutional violence that influence us all, and eventually move past blame to an ethic of justice and practice of care. Conflict is unavoidable, is often healthy and is never truly *solved* by violence. Violence is avoidable and when it isn't avoided, it represents a great lack within our humanity. When we examine this lack and are responsible for it, then we can find ways to strengthen our communities and live in peace.

When someone resorts to violence he or she abdicates such unique human attributes as imagination and creativity, and reveals the limitations of his or her social skills and ability to be in relationship. A culture of peace depends on a holistic world view—one that addresses the continuum of violence as it affects the personal and local conditions of our lives and the interrelatedness of these spheres to the political and global contexts of secrecy, militarism and colonialism.

Trust has become a major creative challenge to building community. Removing suspicion calls for great courage and risk. But demonizing one's adversaries has greater costs. Perhaps, as Arnold Mindell suggests, *it will help if we all listen to women's voices and realize that they are speaking about feelings that we all have.*[6] Nonviolent activism in our communities calls us to help each other heal, our sisters and brothers, sons and daughters, mothers and fathers. The time has certainly come to end transgenerational cycles of violence and give our sons and daughters an awareness of their dignity by modelling nonviolent practices in all our relationships.

> TO TRULY LEARN WHO WE ARE, WE HAVE TO TURN TO ONE ANOTHER AGAIN. WE DO NOT BELONG TO OTHERS, BUT OUR LIVES ARE LINKED; WE BELONG IN A CIRCLE OF OTHERS. WE LEARN BEST TO LISTEN TO OUR OWN VOICES IF WE ARE LISTENING AT THE SAME TIME TO OTHER WOMEN— WHOSE STORIES, FOR ALL OUR DIFFERENCES, TURN OUT, IF WE LISTEN WELL, TO BE OUR STORIES TOO.
> —BARBARA DEMING

3. Alliance-building

We gain strength and power with each other by overcoming our alienation and crossing over to one another with welcoming gestures. Alliance-building between men and women, between majority and minority groups, between religious and secular groups, professionals and laypeople is an exercise in understanding that we are only as powerful as the person next to us. Community models can reach through the gap of large numbers of women and men who are in need of helpers. A feminist community model of nonviolence works from the premise that we can all be helpers. We are all needed to participate in the transformation of violence.

> MY HOPE IS THAT OUR LIVES WILL DECLARE THIS MEETING OPEN.
> —JUNE JORDAN

Transformational change depends on a community finding its own way of getting access to resources for nonviolent change. Positive community conflict resolution and healing respects the uniqueness of each individual, including his or her traditions and needs. Everyone is viewed as a potential resource.

In *Piecing It Together*, Pam McAllister writes that,

> the strength of nonviolent and feminist vision lies in the fact that we do not rely on leaders and elites but on the courage and determination of ordinary people to begin to run their own lives and to work for a world that is possible for everyone.[7]

BUT I HAVE FOUND MY WORK TO BE FAR MORE EFFECTIVE WHEN I START FROM THE PREMISE THAT THE CHANGE, IDEAS AND STRATEGIES APPROPRIATE TO A SITUATION ARE IMBEDDED IN THE CULTURE OR GROUP INVOLVED, WAITING TO BE UNCOVERED.

—FRAN PEAVEY

To deepen democratic process and healing, communities need to move away from being under the control and definition of professionals and leaders. It is not so much a task of overthrowing old systems as it is of building new ones. We can learn from traditions of consensus, talking circles, and conflict resolution; traditions which teach patience, generosity, hospitality, friendship, honesty and lovingkindness. Thich Nhat Hahn tells us: *The problem is not really to reconcile but to heal. To heal and to try to look more deeply to see the roots of our suffering, because the suffering continues (everywhere).*[8]

4. Inclusivity and imagination

EVERY WAR AND EVERY CONFLICT BETWEEN HUMANS HAPPENS BECAUSE OF DISAGREEMENT ABOUT NAMES.... JUST BEYOND THE ARGUING THERE IS A LONG TABLE OF COMPANIONSHIP SET, AND WAITING FOR US TO SIT DOWN.

—RUMI

Unless we look to the imagination for help in healing the suffering in our communities we are likely to repeat the errors of the past. The world's "heart disease" requires new ways of thinking and acting for healing to occur. This is possible when we are able to see and hear things with our hearts open. We widen ourselves to possibilities never before imagined. We become "non-local" in our work in that we readjust our political lens to view our participation in the world as an exploration of extending community beyond the linear logic of subject and object to one of unfolding relationships. By observing the community of plants and animals we can deepen our understanding about the continuity of relationships and the immense care needed in all our relations.

Elder communities that have retained tribal wisdom have commonly taught that we can learn a lot from plants and animals, which are systems of kinship that depend on continuity, reciprocity and respect. Learning to live with all life-forms requires believing that all people, plants, fish, birds and animals are our brothers and sisters. Clouds, rock, water, sky, sun and moon are also honored with respect for their place in the world. For many of us this is a leap of consciousness, or more to the point, a groundedness in our relationship to Earth and our respectful place on the food chain. It is a practice of ecological thinking that shifts many of the ways we live and use resources. By extending our vision of caring intimacy to other sentient beings, we enter a way of compassion that endlessly provides our human community with teachings of healing and transformation. We are moved to expand practices of care to all of our surroundings and participate more mindfully with all of life.

Creative compassion that arises from an expanded ecology of care brings restoration—not because it is complicated or lofty, but because it allows the gift of simplicity to emerge through spontaneous gestures that flow from a generosity of heart unimpeded by hidden agendas. We reach to retrieve what has been exiled inside and out. It is a liberation from persecution that transforms adversaries into protectors by becoming aware of their pain and need for belonging. In Gandhian terms, we realize who we are through selfless action and the identification with those in our communities (local and global) who are suffering, tyrant and victim alike. This form of compassion becomes nonviolent because it steps across boundaries of duality.

We resist tyranny through nonviolent action based on a refusal to harm back. When we try not to harm, the imagination can invoke genuine willingness to bring peace in a spirit of truth and equanimity. We see all things as equal, therefore we treat all things as equal. We see all things as being in need of protection from violence, therefore we are nonviolent with all things. Human rights and justice work develops out of a compassion that is direct in its anger and responses to suffering. And this compassion grows larger when it is extended to the right of all living communities to live without domination. We exclude no species.

Creative action is a constant revolution taking place within the heart and our communities. It replaces persecution, whenever possible, with protection and solidarity. In this kind of revolution, enemies become allies because harm is understood as harm to all and in this, a transformation of intention and action is possible. What kind of mercy brings this kind of transformation? Surely, it is a mercy in which grown men and women show a fearlessness in their capacity for gentleness. And it is a mercy that does not deny the fierceness of a protective and angry love. Certainly, it is a humbler approach to intimacy and all its unknowns. It is not self-absorption but an absorption with the relatedness of all life-forms. Yet we can't forget to include ourselves in the arms of this

OUR TASK MUST BE TO FREE OURSELVES FROM THIS PRISON BY WIDENING OUR CIRCLE OF UNDERSTANDING AND COMPASSION TO EMBRACE ALL LIVING CREATURES AND THE WHOLE OF NATURE IN ITS BEAUTY.

—*ALBERT EINSTEIN*

THERE IS ONLY ONE PRACTISE/

SEEING THE WORLD WHOLE/ AND ALL BEINGS

—*JOANNE THORVALDSON*

compassion either. We begin practising mercy with the self and move from there to the larger community.

5. Consensus

In Western culture we have relied strongly on the rights of the individual. Today, in private households, public communities and global councils there is movement toward more unified statements and actions that honor many different sides of issues and the diversity within our lives. One of the major traditions of nonviolence that can be incorporated into communities and homes is that of consensus. Consensus within First Nations traditions has been practised for a millennia or more and by the Society of Friends (Quakers) for around three hundred years.

CONSENSUS IS BASED ON THE BELIEF THAT EACH PERSON HAS SOME PART OF THE TRUTH, AND NO ONE HAS ALL OF IT, NO MATTER HOW WE WOULD LIKE TO BELIEVE OTHERWISE; AND A RESPECT FOR ALL PERSONS INVOLVED IN THE DECISION THAT IS BEING CONSIDERED.
—CAROLINE ESTES

The feminist movement gave other social change movements an awareness of how personal interaction and group process determine the health and meaningfulness of social change. This awareness teaches that we must leave behind the old adage "the end justifies the means" and focus on how groups can best accomplish goals of unity when the power is decentralized through non-hierarchical organizational structures. This is a tenet of feminist philosophy that has merged with the principles of a variety of nonviolent traditions such as those found in Quaker and some First Nations community processes. Integral to feminist traditions of consensus is the recognition of all contributions of participants, the valuing of co-operation over competition, and the basic premise that nonviolence begins in the way we treat each other and all our relationships.

Consensus arises from principles of unity that develop from basic agreements used to help define the working relationship of the group. These agreements depend on the readiness of each participant to carry the workload, an openness to hear new ideas and a willingness to change. Consensus is a process where a decision is the result of deep synthesis and consideration of the ideas of every member in the group. No decision is concluded until everyone in the group feels comfortable with the decision.

Decisions reached by consensus are arrived at through a format of speaking in rounds, deep listening, questioning, discussing, proposing, modifying, amending and unifying. Trust in consensus process is central to its strength, trust that grows out of knowing where each other stands and sharing knowledge in non-dominating and therefore, often empowering ways. In some instances, periods of silence are used when differences are no longer opened up to inquiry and exploration and a time of reflection is needed to restore a sense of respect and trust.

Risk-taking, gentle humor, humility, endurance, commitment and faith in the group's ability to reach consensus are qualities of participants which often contribute to group success. When people in a consensus-based group are open to transforming ideas, intentions and actions, then transformation is likely to happen and the results are rarely what is expected. In this regard, preconceived notions of decisions usually hamper the creative potential of the process and diminish the power within an individual to act co-operatively with all participants. The power of consensus processes to arrive at unforeseen decisions is in the beauty of an inclusive and far-reaching vision; this vision is formed when participants are fully present and committed to finding practical solutions.

Controversial issues particularly benefit from a consensus process when groups are fractured into entrenched and seemingly unmoveable positions. Consensus seeks to uproot rigidity into fluid possibilities. Dichotomies of win/lose, either/or are replaced with alternatives based on win-win goals and both-and solutions. Differences inform and expand consciousness, creating feedback loops that are positive and integrative.

In consensus process there is ultimately a gathering of truth and energy until a common answer emerges. When agreement emerges, a decision is self-evident and usually felt by all. It may not necessarily be unanimous but it is one which all can stand beside, or aside, and move ahead with. Blocking or holding a group from moving ahead is rare and is often contingent on feeling a moral wrongness with the decision. As Caroline Estes stated in "Consensus and Community," an interview published in *Turtle Talk: Voices for a Sustainable Future*: "It's very rare that any of us has the audacity to think that we have more wisdom than the collected wisdom of the group. And when those occasions occur, it is very difficult for us to take that stand. You must be *terribly* sure."[9]

There are a number of excellent resources for learning consensus. Some of these manuals and books are recommended in the Selected Reading section of this book and stand as wonderful examples of developing nonviolent process in our communities.

OF ALL THESE MODES OF DECISION-MAKING, CONSENSUS DEPENDS ON GOOD WILL AND A POSITIVE ATTITUDE.
—B.C. ROUNDTABLE ON SUSTAINABLE LAND USE

A GOOD CONSENSUS DECISION OUGHT TO MAKE US SAY, "THAT IS WHAT I REALLY WANTED, BUT I DID NOT REALIZE IT."

CONSENSUS DECISION-MAKING IS NOT ABOUT COMPROMISE, IT'S ABOUT FINDING THE BEST DECISION BY HEARING ALL PARTS OF THE TRUTH.

A CLASH OF DOCTRINES IS NOT A DISASTER, IT'S AN OPPORTUNITY.
—HOWARD BRINTON

At the heart of all consensus is making sure that everyone has the power to contribute from the beginning to the end of the process. Consensus avoids the exclusivity that is often at the root of decisions that create unrest and inequality. Consensus is efficient and effective. It demonstrates decision-making that is only possible within the completeness of collective unity based on common purpose and genuine understanding.

6. Community efforts

There are many examples of nonviolent action in national and international communities. There are also smaller community efforts, ranging from informal networking and groups to larger campaigns and projects, which are examples of imaginative service defined by the resources that are specific to the community doing the organizing.

THE IMPORTANT THING IS TO AWAKEN A CRITICAL CONSCIOUSNESS IN THE BASIC COMMUNITIES, SO THEY CAN FIND THEIR OWN SOLUTIONS TO THEIR PROBLEMS.

—Adolfo Perez Esquiel

In a small British Columbia community called Argenta, a group of people have been meeting weekly for many years to write protest and peace letters on behalf of those around the world who are suffering from human rights violations. Nearby in Kaslo, after a community course on nonviolence in 1991, a group of women and men continued meeting. They saw the need to continue inquiry into the daily content of their lives, particularly hoping to move further from isolating and cynical patterns into life-affirming and community-linking contexts based on simple gestures of weekly pot-luck suppers and friendship. Nonviolence there has been practised by aiding those who were freeing themselves from abusive relationships, celebrating and sharing diversity, and supporting neighbors in work, at home and in the community.

We can learn also from the development of Buddhist sanghas or communities of practitioners such as those arising from the Tiep Hien tradition—a tradition that, through Buddhism, combines social action with the individual practice of peace. Thich Nhat Hahn, a Buddhist monk and teacher who founded the Tiep Hien Order with other Buddhist monks and nuns during the Vietnam War, has spent many decades teaching the experience of interconnection with all life. He believes we "can sustain social change work far better than righteous partisanship."[10] During the 1960s he founded the Youth for Social Services and an underground network of Buddhist social workers in his homeland Vietnam to assist homeless, hungry and injured villagers on both sides of the

TRANSFORMING COLLECTIVE CONSCIOUSNESS IS THE ONLY WAY TO MAKE PEACE, TO PREVENT WAR.

—Thich Nhat Hahn

war. Out of these efforts grew a non-monastic order called Tiep Hien. The teachings, as they have come to be known in the West, are called *Interbeing* and are represented in fourteen precepts. They are helpful for bridging the dichotomy between violence and nonviolence because of the way they uniquely deal with contemporary issues through personal and social action for peace.

In the introduction to Thich Nhat Hahn's book *Interbeing*, Fred Eppsteiner remarks how at a time when the land and people of Vietnam "were being destroyed in the name of supposedly irreconcilable 'isms,' the Order was acutely aware of the need for all people to realize the commonality of their experience and to renounce all views that posited the One Truth or One Way."[11] Fanaticism, religious and political self-righteousness are directly rejected by the first three precepts. The fourth precept asks that a practice of compassion go to the heart of suffering by direct involvement, by work in our communities that addresses the social conditions of people's lives. This is realized through the fifth and sixth precepts, which teach that nonviolence can develop through work that is in alignment with our principles and an understanding of the interdependent contexts of anger and abuse: "If I had been born in the social conditions of a [rapist] and raised like a [rapist], then I would be a [rapist] now.[12] The interdependent causes of rape makes it the individual's as well as society's responsibility.

Guidelines for peaceful living are already alive in our communities, waiting for us to use them. They are ways of learning peace that have equivalents in all our spiritual traditions wherever the way is open to direct action, transformation and healing. *We do not know everything. But we can minimize our ignorance.*[13] If we learn together then we will develop trust as we work, and become more joyful. Often, as Thich Nhat Hahn has taught, "if we look deeply, we will observe that the roots of war are in the unmindful ways we have been living."[14] We can support each other in developing mindfulness.

TO PREVENT THE NEXT WAR, WE HAVE TO PRACTICE PEACE TODAY. IF WE WAIT UNTIL ANOTHER WAR IS IMMINENT TO BEGIN TO PRACTICE, IT WILL BE TOO LATE.
—THICH NHAT HAHN

Let us begin creating heart-sharing groups, nonviolence study groups, parent-support groups, recovery circles, meditation practices, bioregional congresses where we can be practitioners of hope, strength and action. Let us be fair witnesses to the suffering in our community and consider committees of care in the tradition of Quakers. Let us begin to imagine and organize, in the tradition of Peace Brigades International and the Duluth Model of

Intervention, "peace-witness" groups of citizens who are specifically trained in nonviolence and careful observation; they can visit homes where violence is occurring in order to document the violence and assist the healing needs of every family member. Let us support class actions that address powerfully the structural forms of violence that perpetuate the systematic, socially sanctioned brutality of women's lives. Let us draw from the holistic world view of feminists, which offers a conceptualization of peace and stimulation of a process that is on the cutting edge of linking development with disarmament, and peace education with changing the culture of violence.

Nonviolence needs to be incorporated into our daily lives before we will see global change. We begin by addressing the personal, women and men and children together, by caring for our own lives. This reverberates throughout the globe of which we are all a part. Nonviolence means women and men are reconciled with themselves and nature by conspiring to care for this world rather than destroy it. This calls for immense courage and strength. It requires we keep our hearts, homes and communities open, allow the wounds to heal and continue to reach for, to learn about, and to practice peace.

THERE IS CAUSE FOR GREAT ALARM, BUT THERE IS A GREATER NEED FOR THOUGHTFUL ACTION.

—W. J. MUSA MOORE-FOSTER

Notes

[1] Rosalinda Ramirez, in *Common Ground: Love, Justice, Truth, Spirituality* Vol. VI (Richmond, Indiana, 1992), p. 6.

[2] Arnold Mindell, *The Leader As Martial Artist* (San Francisco: Harper, 1992), p. 119.

[3] CBC News, August 28, 1993.

[4] Charlene Spretnak, *States of Grace* (San Francisco: Harper, 1991), p. 74.

[5] Arnold Mindell, *The Leader as Martial Artist*, p. 101.

[6] Ibid., p. 123.

[7] Pam McAllister, *Piecing It Together: Feminism and Nonviolence* (London, U.K.: Feminism and Nonviolence Study Group in co-operation with the War Resisters' International, 1983), p. 30.

[8] Catherine Ingram, *In the Footsteps of Gandhi: Conversations With Spiritual Social Activists* (Berkeley, CA: Parallax Press, 1990), p. 85.

[9] Plant, Christopher & Judith, *Turtle Talk: Voices for a Sustainable Future*, (Gabriola Island & Philadelphia: New Society Publishers,

1990), p. 96.

[10] See Joanna Macy's essay in *Healing the Wounds* (Philadelphia & Gabriola Island: New Society Publishers, 1989), p. 208.

[11] (Berkeley, CA: Parallax Press, 1987), p. 6.

[12] See Thich Nhat Hahn, *Interbeing*, p. 39. I have inserted rapist for sea-pirate.

[13] Thich Nhat Hahn, *For a Future to Be Possible: Commentaries on the Five Wonderful Precepts* (Berkeley, CA: Parallax Press, 1993), p. 11.

[14] Ibid., p. 15.

OUR FUTURE

XII CREATIVE JUSTICE

1. Our commonality

Our present international legal and political systems are overwhelmed by processes which are beyond the determination of "the truth," who is right and wrong. The elder in us knows there is no final equity in blunt adversarial conflict. A sense of justice arises only in connection with community, with inner peace of mind, sustainable ongoing relationship, and worldwork that processes the tensions between groups.

—*Arnold Mindell*

Nonviolence is a process. It is a way of becoming free of mental anguish and the control or division that commonly rules our lives. Basic to all nonviolent practice is the effort to overcome inner division and to liberate the truth. This involves shaping our life story with awareness and non-attachment. Awareness is bringing close attention to how we live our lives. Non-attachment is placing more importance on the questions than on our answers. It is recognizing the process of change as being open and ongoing.

Bringing nonviolence into communities is not a linear process. It is a process whereby each step opens into another, creating new forms as it evolves. There is no one strategy or final solution; each community needs to look closely at the resources already at hand and begin with faith that the tools we need are already with us. These tools are the ingenuity, determination and basic living skills we all have. Our commonality can bind us together in nonviolent efforts to create safe homes and communities. If we can allow the ways in which we address violence to stay open and imaginative, justice work becomes creative.

Creative justice work begins from the premise that community needs to be cherished in light of each individual's uniqueness. It is important to begin to bring this approach to victims and perpetrators of violence with the awareness that the healing needs of each are determined by the particular characteristics, culture and courage of that person. Traditionally, we have responded to violence with generalized punishment and blame, ignoring the specialness of each person. It is time we looked closely at the systems that prevent responses based on accountability, humanity and equanimity.

Before we can face the truth of personal trauma in another, we need to sit down with ourselves and see the suffering caused in our resistance to fear, anger, despair and hope. This book has focused deeply on this aspect of nonviolence process. We can begin to help each other heal when we understand that the continuum of violence runs through "the landscapes of all our hearts."

Creative justice (or any justice) is impossible without the belief that there is a place for everyone in our communities. If we continue to exclude, disbelieve, persecute and misunderstand those who suffer from living in violent relationships, be it victim or offender, we will continue the division and hate that feeds violent behavior. Our repulsion of violence is both a help and a hindrance. Our repulsion is real and clearly warns us that the harm taking place is terrible. Our repulsion can also prevent us from being responsive to the needs of those trapped in abusive cycles. There are ways for each of us to be inside rather than outside our communities, to find our place and simple ways of contributing and receiving.

> MIRACLES SEEM TO REST, NOT SO MUCH UPON FACES OR VOICES OR HEALING POWER COMING SUDDENLY NEAR TO US FROM FAR OFF, BUT UPON OUR PERCEPTIONS BEING MADE FINER SO THAT FOR A MOMENT OUR EYES CAN SEE AND OUR EARS CAN HEAR THAT WHICH IS ABOUT US ALWAYS.
> —WILLA CATHER

2. Prosecution and persecution

Our criminal justice system is slowly beginning to treat the issue of violence against women with some seriousness. For the most part though, *the law sees and treats women the way men see and treat women.*[1] We have laws against assault. The criminal justice system is responsible for law enforcement. Legislation accomplishes little until the police and judicial systems are trained and prepared to follow through with prosecution and protection. *Prosecution* of the offender is a necessary step for the crime to be fully acknowledged and retribution made possible. *Protection* of the victim is necessary to save lives and can't be left to police discretion; it must be provided without deliberation. When a protection or restraining order exists, it is the state responsibility to protect the individual. When state protection fails, judiciary and government process is failing. Jurisprudence then is not realized and more women are killed.

> WE CAN BEST HELP YOU TO PREVENT WAR NOT BY REPEATING YOUR WORDS AND FOLLOWING YOUR METHODS BUT BY FINDING NEW WORDS AND CREATING NEW METHODS.
> —VIRGINIA WOOLF

Without a proper judicial process for dealing with domestic violence, intervention easily becomes regressive and not supportive of institutional, cultural and personal change. When there are no consequences, there is systemic support for abusive men to become more dangerous and hurt more women and children. Male murder of women in North America is on the rise. Every month, more than 50,000 U.S. women seek restraining or protection orders.[2] The absence of prosecution condones violence against women and children. *At every point in the process, the victim must be heard and cared for.* Otherwise, the process of victimization continues and the victim is denied safety and recovery, and an offender is denied responsibility and reformation. Re-victimizing a victim of abuse and battering through habits of denial and neglect feeds the continuum of violence.

FOR WE HAVE, BUILT INTO ALL OF US, OLD BLUEPRINTS OF EXPECTATION AND RESPONSE, OLD STRUCTURES OF OPPRESSION, AND THESE MUST BE ALTERED AT THE SAME TIME WE ALTER THE LIVING CONDITIONS WHICH ARE A RESULT OF THOSE STRUCTURES. FOR THE MASTER'S TOOLS WILL NEVER DISMANTLE THE MASTER'S HOUSE.
    —AUDRE LORDE

A response by the criminal justice system, however, does not solve the larger issue if *persecution* continues to disable both victim and offender. As citizens we need to assist the criminal justice system in stopping violence against women by taking responsibility for the problem at a grassroots level. One way to do this is to build community responses that are non-adversarial. Community responses are effective when they are built on premises of deep democracy and grace, wherein public life is viewed not only as secular but also as sacred.

The criminal justice system is not the answer to our problems. It is a temporary and external aspect of transforming violence that must serve to strengthen justice, the protection of victims and the unacceptability of violence. We cannot expect a patriarchal system steeped in corporate economics to provide the reform or healing so needed on a deeper and more integrative level, but it certainly must be part of the reform.

Transformation happens when all parts of society turn toward the misery and marginalization that a culture of violence produces: legislators, prosecutors and citizens together laying down a path of nonviolence as we individually and collectively learn to walk a deeper democracy.

3. Deep democracy

Democratic practices that come from deep within the heart are practices that are beyond blame. Deep democracy works to open the closed systems that imprison the emotional and spiritual wisdom we need in order to be socially responsible. Deep democracy sees that there are no sides. Instead, it understands violence as a continuum of which we are all a part.

Processing conflict must become an accepted and ongoing part of community. Conflict resolution processes need to build on self-awareness that is generated by a vision of wholeness. Without a vision of wholeness in which healing is possible for all, we continue to disenfranchise aspects of ourselves and individuals in our communities. Deep democracy makes life worthwhile but, as Arnold Mindell says, it does not rid ourselves of conflict as much as does bringing awareness to how we work with that conflict:

> What appears from one viewpoint to be a disastrous problem, illness, or conflict unfolds from another viewpoint and reveals itself as an awesome opportunity.[3]

Deep democracy touches upon all levels of our lives. In personal life, it means openness to all of our inner voices, feelings and movements, not just the ones we know and support, but also the ones we fear and do not know well. In relationships, deep democracy means having ongoing awareness of our highest ideals and worst moods. In group life it means the willingness to listen to and experiment with whatever comes up. In global work, deep democracy values politics, ethnicity, separatism and the spirit of nature.[4]

The threat of violence to us offers the potential for profoundly creative nonviolent action. It calls for a deeper democracy. It calls us to be visionaries, risk-takers and firm believers in a new paradigm based on wholeness, fluidity and reconciliation.

Deep democracy believes every human being is of equal importance and has a special calling or *a meaningful response to our larger self and the grandeur of the ongoing story.*[5] Deep democrats arouse people from apathy and make them think. And they often do this more through action than words. Peace Pilgrim was an example of this.[6] Who are these people in your own community? Deep democracy sees the potential in everyone to be a leader because of its realization that everyone is needed to fully represent reality. It is a false belief that we can isolate ourselves in our prejudices and survive as self-sufficient world systems. All our relationships are interdependent. We will not have economic or sexual democracy until we can create a true democracy where all human beings are treated as equal and integral to the whole. This involves recovery of the female and male role of being Elders in our communities, *where elders practising deep democracy will expect and even invite disturbers into the circle before they become terrorists.*[7] As Jack Ross put it in *Nonviolence for Elfin Spirits:*

> Relationships take precedence over getting and keeping power, reputation and honor. Rather than conquering enemies one hopes for transformation, turning opponents into friends and allies to deal with common problems.[8]

OLD SYSTEMS OF EXPLOITATION AND OPPRESSION ARE PASSING AWAY; NEW SYSTEMS OF JUSTICE AND EQUALITY ARE BEING BORN. IN A REAL SENSE THIS IS A GREAT TIME TO BE ALIVE.
—MARTIN LUTHER KING JR.

WITH EVERY TRUE FRIENDSHIP WE BUILD MORE FIRMLY FOUNDATIONS UPON WHICH THE PEACE OF THE WHOLE WORLD RESTS.
—MAHATMA GANDHI

It is a deep commitment to coming together to learn about each other sufficiently to bridge the chasms that separate us. Peace Pilgrim taught that only by working for the good of the whole can we relinquish the destructive cycle of alienation. She suggests the following steps:

1. *right attitude toward life (bringing awareness);*
2. *bringing our lives into harmony with the natural laws that govern this universe;*
3. *believing each of us has a special place in the life pattern; and*
4. *simplifying our lives so clarity of being is more possible and we make room for community work.*[9]

4. A third way

At a San Francisco anti-nuclear rally in 1982, a powerful activist and writer of our time, Alice Walker, delivered the following words:

> I intend to protect my home. Praying—not a curse—only the hope that my courage will not fail my love. But if by some miracle, and all our struggle, the Earth is spared, only justice to every living thing (and everything is alive) will save humankind.
>
> And we are not saved yet.
>
> *Only justice can stop a curse.*[10]

In much of her work there is a call for justice that is removed from the dispirited pessimism of non-redemptive despair. This call is a fine and durable thread stitched through Walker's and many other feminist's work with an intelligence that is perpetually *open* to transformation. This is an intelligence that cultivates life, that lends itself to forms of power that work with and for others. It is love that is abundant and increasing in joy. It is an intelligence that is spacious and organic in its logic, unpredictable in its nature, and precise in its rage. And not stopping here, it is self-defining in its voice and often, bold in its beauty. As Robin Morgan writes, it is about transformation which

> requires that we recognize our own just anger as being so vast that mere violence could not possibly address it. Transformation requires more than mere seeing; it requires all forms of perception, including remembering, imagining, intuiting, hallucinating, dreaming and empathizing. And transformation requires that we *act*, that we *step off the wheel, outside the prescribed boundaries altogether.*[11]

IF WE CAN RECOGNIZE THAT CHANGE AND UNCERTAINTY ARE BASIC PRINCIPLES, WE CAN GREET THE FUTURE AND THE TRANSFORMATION WE ARE UNDERGOING WITH THE UNDERSTANDING THAT WE DO NOT KNOW ENOUGH TO BE PESSIMISTIC. THE LIFE FORCE WITHIN EACH OF US CAN THEN FOCUS ON THE POSSIBLE AND THE POTENTIALITIES.

—HAZEL HENDERSON

Many activists and writers are giving us works of creative justice that perceive and practice forms of power which have the ability to open up unforeseen possibilities of transformation. This is power that restores hope, heals wounds, rebuilds villages and imagines justice "to every living thing." And it is strongly pragmatic; all will be fed as we change the economy of food for the few to an ecology of care and a redefinition of growth and productivity.

There is an unstoppable desire for life. Creative justice work is multidimensional; it has a natural tendency against doing things in one or two ways or defining difference in terms of dichotomy. Creative justice politics resounds with a third way. This is an epistemology that I hear named by Robin Morgan as an *erotic intelligence* or the *politics of eros*; by Mary Daly as *biophilic* or life-loving; by Julia Kristeva as a *democracy of the multiple*; Riane Eisler as a *partnership model of society*; and Fran Peavey as *heart politics*. This list goes on, as does an invention of life without the death-politics of dominator cultures; it is a naming that continues as it creates itself.

> MY HEART IS MOVED BY ALL I CANNOT SAVE; SO MUCH HAS BEEN DESTROYED. I HAVE TO CAST MY LOT WITH THOSE WHO AGE AFTER AGE, PERVERSELY, WITH NO EXTRAORDINARY POWER, RECONSTITUTE THE WORLD.
>
> —ADRIENNE RICH

A third form of politics steps outside patriarchal law, dominator mentalities, and politically motivated economics. A third way engages power not from the predominant individualistic theories of monopolizing growth, but power that increases nonviolent consciousness through its tendency for dynamic harmlessness and helpfulness. It is a multiplicity of feminisms, where distinctions are honored and differences are welcomed, and each is endlessly allowed its full expression. In fact, in this third way we do well to pay attention to how we define labor and love, and take cues from those traditions that learn to see working relationships as engaged in "the dance of life."

In this politic we are building "beloved communities" wherever we go. We are unafraid of the power that links rather than ranks, that is moving from a patriarchal and monolithic society to one of partnership and pluralism. It is where the concepts of *foreigner* and *border* become obsolete because strangeness is no longer viewed as a threat. Nationalistic tendencies give way to tolerance and hospitality, religious morality to spiritual health, a single-market economy to ecological sanity, and otherness to familiarity. Issues of individual rights and community/collective responsibilities are understood as inseparable. Yes, there are contradictions in a third

> THERE IS PLACE BETWEEN DREAMING AND LIVING, A THIRD WAY. GUESS IT.
>
> —ANTONIO MACHADO

possibility; but contradiction is not strangled in a grip of aggressive hegemony. Rather, contradiction is looked upon for the paradoxical, hence revealing, nature it offers.

Women begin from a place of marginality. Perhaps this is the "motor of change."[12] As Robin Morgan tells us,

> If for centuries women have been accused by the Right of being dangerously radical creatures and by the Left of being dangerously conservative ones, it is because the sub-patriarchal reality in which women live is a third politics altogether. That is the reality now starting to manifest in the "world of appearances."[13]

This is a politic in which we surprise ourselves and others with courage and change. We maintain a vision of a culture without its forms of imperialistic, soul-defying violence and continue to find in our multiple truths an ecstasy of living that has never found reason in war, or sanity in the prevention of women from full participation in the world. A world without violence is conceivable in a third politics, as we revolt against all forms of sexual slavery and refuse to stifle reverence for all life.

A third politic will, *if we choose it* and *if we are willing to act on it,* transform the culture of violence affecting us all. It is a necessary revolt that takes place inside our individual psyches as well as outside in community action. A third politic takes place on many levels at once. It is making ourselves present. It is freeing the unconscious from its prison of delusion and shifting our identities to an existence that exclaims itself with joy, and because of this naturally attracts many to its way. This is a wakefulness that understands our birthright as women, as any human being, as one of thriving, not just striving.[14]

> So it is not merely the absence of war but the presence of peace, not merely the absence of tragedy but the presence of comedy, not merely the absence of hate but the presence of love, not merely the absence of ignorance but the presence of intelligence, not merely the absence of death but the presence of life. And it is not merely the absence of fear, but the presence of trust.[15]

How can we not, women and men, be drawn to such a presence?

Do I CONTRADICT MYSELF?
VERY WELL THEN, I CONTRADICT MYSELF.
I AM LARGE, I CONTAIN MULTITUDES.

—WALT WHITMAN

SURELY ALL OF US ARE NERVED BY ONE ANOTHER, CATCH COURAGE FROM ONE ANOTHER.

—BARBARA DEMING

5. Four-fold way

In closing this section on creative justice I would like to include the work of Angeles Arrien on personal accountability. I have found the steps she recommends helpful in most personal and community conflict processes. The four-fold way is based on Arrien's cross-cultural studies of universal values common to all humanity. They are useful in any situation and are as follows:

NO PEACE WITHOUT TRUTH.

NO POWER, ONLY LOVE.

—JOANNE THORVALDSON

1. *Show-up*: The way of the warrior accesses the resources of power and presence.
2. *Speak the truth without blame and judgment*: The way of the visionary accesses the resources of vision, intuition and authenticity.
3. *Pay attention to what has heart and meaning*: The way of the healer accesses the resources of love, gratitude, acknowledgement and validation.
4. *Be open to outcome, not attached to outcome*: The way of the teacher accesses the resources of wisdom and creativity.[16]

Notes

[1] Catherine MacKinnon, "Feminism, Marxism, Method and the State: Toward Feminist Jurisprudence," *Signs* 8:2 (1983), p. 644.

[2] See Anne Jones, *Next Time, She'll Be Dead* (1994) and "No More! Stopping Domestic Violence," *Ms.* V:2 (September/October, 1994) for overview and up-to-date statistics. Page 6 and 46 respectively for above quotes.

[3] Arnold Mindell, *The Leader As Martial Artist: An Introduction to Deep Democracy* (San Francisco: Harper, 1992), p. 151.

[4] Ibid., pp. 154-5.

[5] Charlene Spretnak, *States of Grace: The Recovery of Meaning in a Postmodern Age* (New York: HarperCollins, 1991).

[6] From 1953 until her death in 1981, Peace Pilgrim walked more than 25,000 miles across the U.S. spreading her message of peace. Her pilgrimage covered the entire peace picture: peace among nations, groups, individuals, and the very important inner peace—because that is where peace begins. She believed that world peace would come when enough people attained inner peace.

[7] Arnold Mindell, *The Leader As Martial Artist*, p. 157.

[8] Argenta Friends Press, 1992, p. 68.

[9] *Steps Toward Inner Peace: Harmonious Principles for Human Living*

(Hemet, California: Friends of Peace Pilgrim).

[10] Quoted from *Reweaving the Web of Life: Feminism and Nonviolence*, ed. Pam McAllister (Philadelphia & Gabriola Island: New Society Publishers, 1982), p. 265.

[11] *The Demon Lover: On the Sexuality of Terrorism* (New York: W.W. Norton, 1989), p. 328.

[12] Julia Kristera, "An interview with Julia Kristera: Cultural Strangeness and the Subject in Crisis," by Suzanne Clark and Kathleen Hulley in *Discourse*, Fall-Winter, 1990-91. See *Strangers to Ourselves*, trans. Leon Rondiez (New York: Columbia Press, 1991).

[13] *The Demon Lover*, p. 327.

[14] See Clarissa Pinkola Estés, *Women Who Run With the Wolves* (New York: Ballantine, 1992), p. 198.

[15] Robin Morgan, *The Demon Lover*, p. 341.

[16] Angeles Arrien, *The Four-Fold Way: Walking the Paths of Warrior, Teacher, Healer and Visionary* (San Francisco: Harper, 1992).

XIII GRACE

1. Dream of the other

Transformation takes some kind of crazy wisdom. The craziness of love without fear. And the wisdom of love without harm. Yet, we are so divided against ourselves; as Gary Snyder says it, "Our immediate business, and our quarrel, is with ourselves."[1] We see plants, animals, even other human beings as separate from ourselves. We forget to hold sameness and difference as equally valuable. Instead, we lose ourselves in comparison, condemnation and conditional love: all eventually leading to self-hate and the development of an enemy-based consciousness. We easily forget the gift we have been given in our capacity to breathe and move freely. We forget to create rituals that celebrate the gift of living. We need courtesy and ceremony, responsibility and renewal. We need each other.

PROCEED FROM THE DREAM OUTWARD.
—CARL JUNG

Celebration of the living sources around us is often realized through practices of gratitude. These practices have no rules; they are often simple and common gestures of thanks. Anything goes; when the gesture is rooted in the heart and acknowledges more than self, there is often an opening into grace. Gratitude is an acknowledgement of the "other" in our life or that which resides alongside ourselves—the breathing presence of other life-forms. It is a soulful experience when we realize the sacredness of this planet's living process. The soul, in this sense, is often likened to a psyche or presence larger than ourselves. Gary Snyder said it well when he wrote, *Our "soul" is our dream of the other.*[2]

ALL THAT I KNOW SPEAKS TO ME THROUGH THE EARTH, AND I LONG TO TELL YOU, YOU WHO ARE EARTH TOO, AND LISTEN AS WE SPEAK TO EACH OTHER OF WHAT WE KNOW: THE LIGHT IS IN US.
—SUSAN GRIFFIN

2. Relationship as a sacrament

It is possible to extend ourselves more and more into and with the larger presence of the world. We do this through peaceful relationship and a genuine effort to understand each other. Relationship is a sacrament. Its grace is the stories it tells, the opportunities for healing it provides, and the freedom it offers.

Relationship cannot be possessed, no matter how hard we may try to do so. It is an impermanent and fluid process of change. We cannot take any final hold of relationship but we can love it, enduringly, in all its paradox, craziness and uncertainty.

Living with each other and all species takes great care if we wish to include the spirit of *ahimsa* or non-harming. When we take life for food, it is important we do so mindfully and thankfully—that we are aware of the life energy we are growing, consuming, harvesting and killing. We are responsible for protecting all life sources. We do this when we alter our habits of consumption and simplify to conserve balance and ensure far-reaching care for generations of species to follow. These species are dependent on how we choose to live with all our relations today.

3. Forgiveness

More than taking away from this planet and each other, we need to be for giving—giving to ourselves and others what is really needed. Women and men need to find for ourselves our gifts and ways of realizing how to be in gentle relationship with all beings, beginning with ourselves. If we are to give to ourselves the possibility of healing in ways that bring wholeness and unity, we must surrender to the healing being asked of all of us. We must be for the giving of this kind of life—taking care of the sacred life energy within ourselves by honoring what we need to say and do, or not say and not do, in order to prevent harming ourselves and others. We need to care for our woundedness so we can find ways of living through joy rather than pain.

This kind of giving is often distorted in a theology of forgiveness that denies the true needs of the victims and perpetrators. No one should be asked to forgive an abuser. The healing that begins to return some of the life energy stolen by one who is already alienated and broken occurs when an abuser accepts responsibility for having been abusive, stops the abuse and asks what form of retribution is needed. As Carol J. Adams clearly put it, "Forgiveness in the absence of repentance by the abuser is a salve for the conscience of society, but it is not a healing experience for the victim."[3] And I would add, neither is it healing for the perpetrator, for it prevents the necessary steps of transformation and healing to take place for both. When forgiveness of another occurs, it is most safely an experience that is deeply, and usually privately, defined by a self or society no longer in denial of the injuries experienced and the healing required.

We undo harm by giving in ways that feed and honor the life force within and around us. We advocate for living processes—the growth, change and daily effort of being our true selves. Our true self—the face that showed itself at birth—is never nurtured into wholeness through violence. We are forgiving in the deepest sense when we heal our brokenness and choose an active path of dynamic nonviolence.

4. A conspiracy of love

There is a terrorist trade that is anti-life and militates against the healing of pain. One in which children are being sold for their organs, to "banks" to accommodate the very rich. How many hearts, I wonder? Our children and their hearts colonized for commerce. Perhaps this form of terrorism inflicted on the innocent, and the forms of terror we inflict on ourselves, are a lack of acceptance of pain, which comes from not knowing how to love. A lack that is monstrous, the visible form of a diseased heart.

WHILE YOU HERE DO SNORING LIE,/ OPEN-EYED CONSPIRACY/ HIS TIME DOTH TAKE./ IF OF LIFE YOU KEEP A CARE,/ SHAKE OFF SLUMBER AND BEWARE:/ AWAKE! AWAKE!
—WILLIAM SHAKESPEARE

A conspiracy of love that cannot be bought, controlled or regulated is growing. It calls for a boundless, open heart. This involves the willingness to move from the centre to unsettled and improvised positions, and learn by heart what a non-enemy ethic means in our lives.[4] Can we begin again and again by looking for the spaciousness within a nonviolent heart, wherever we find it? "Deep down," the Dalai Lama says,

> we must have real affection for each other, a clear realization or recognition of our shared human status. At the same time we must openly accept many ideologies and systems as means of solving humanity's problem. One country, one nation, one ideology, is not enough.[5]

Even the most nonviolent traditions lack something, for the problems of division and duality exist everywhere. Boundlessness comes from a whole stream of self seeing without division. Much of what we can do is question how we contribute to the practice of division, and become more open. Only we can be responsible for peaceful action. We cannot do this for someone else.

At the Los Angeles World Affairs Council on Compassion in World Politics, the Dalai Lama spoke about how heart-to-heart contact is needed in order to understand that all humans are the same. He said "the problem of the human heart must first be solved."[6] And "similarly, when we encounter human suffering, it is important to respond with compassion rather than to question the politics of those we help."[7] It is not possible to exist any longer in complete isolation. As quantum physics and natural laws show us, we are bound by our interdependence. But the boundlessness in our hearts is fenced in by the problems we impose on our own ideological differences. It is so simple and yet we bind any loving with the armor of our ideology. How to unbound what we are lacking in our hearts, which exists as a result of our isolation?

THE MIND CREATES THE ABYSS AND THE HEART CROSSES OVER IT. LOVE IS THE BRIDGE.
—STEPHEN LEVINE

The monsters of our love are often those closest to us. They are sometimes a beloved, but they are not often loving. Nonetheless, they reside in our beds, dwell in our psyches and have in common a staked interest in usurping our life force until, as victims, we drop. To subvert the patriarchal plot of putting boundaries on love, of calling love a scarce resource, we create instead a conspiracy to co-exist with all. Being in relation and boundless in love, without harm, requires that we all become law breakers. We need an "open-eyed conspiracy," where choices in love are made with a wide awake presence of self.

5. A bounding heart

A bounding heart requires keen and open eyes and ears. It requires we begin with ourselves, the practice of attentive non-injury, by bounding back into our bodies with the intention to listen. There are so many differences we do not hear, and there are those we do not have the courage to see.[8] How to make new these love-lacking hearts of ours so we do have the courage to hear and see, *each time*, the difference? The bounding heart finds a way in the process of pausing again and again to question our own collaborative attitudes, our distinguishing ourselves as better, and our own ways of locating our truths. Sexual abuse survivors teach that we need to learn to make room for all our truths, even in the form of enemies, in order to speak them and see them for what they are. Do we collaborate with the enemy inside or out by feigning our lack (or our strength) and not seeing the problem for what it is—our lack of love?

FOR SELF IS A SEA BOUNDLESS AND MEASURELESS....
—KAHLIL GIBRAN

Our heartbeat is the sign we are all given to hear the truth we need. Holding one's breath—stilling our hearts in fear so even the trace of our own heartbeat is inaudible—is the first stillness in our body into which we must bring sound. The pure joy of breathing in order to think and act and be awake is a sign we are becoming alive in our efforts. From the Dhammapada:

O let us live in joy, in love amongst those who hate!
Among men who hate, let us live in love.

O let us live in joy, in health amongst those who are ill!
Among men who are ill, let us live in health.

O let us live in joy, in peace amongst those who struggle!
Among men who struggle, let us live in peace.[9]

How many years have you held you breath under the conditions of an oppressive reality? Breathing more fully each time, our hearts take freer leaps that extend into a different kind of breathing—wider, deeper, and gradually, with an awareness of others breathing. A different hearing. That is the difference of a bounding heart—that we purposely choose to hear the other.[10]

KNOW THAT JOY IS RARER, MORE DIFFICULT AND MORE BEAUTIFUL THAN SADNESS. ONCE YOU MAKE THIS ALL-IMPORTANT DISCOVERY, YOU MUST EMBRACE JOY AS A MORAL OBLIGATION.

—ANDRÉ GIDE

6. Joy

Our sexuality has been made a source of division and woundedness. As children we are often taught to feel shame for what is natural and as young adults to exploit what is not ours. Many of us have forgotten to respect the gift of our bodies and have come to view the preciousness of this life force, like so much else, as a commodity. Our eroticism becomes buried in yet another international industry designed to eventually annihilate the very spirit that makes sexual communion joyful in the first place. Pornography is not eroticism and ecstasy; no woman or man knows joy when the soul is in bondage to slavery.

There is a joy that know no division, exploitation or lie. It is the ecstasy of giving or receiving the embrace of another in mutual respect and conscious choice. It is the meeting of two bodies in deep emotional communion. It is the joy our children exhibit running freely with the wind in their hair and the sound of their voice uninhibited. It is laughter that bursts from the depths of a belly in amazing grace, humility or hilarity because of a willingness to see comedy in our delusions. Joy is given birth again and again when we are in the throes of creative process—when the heart,

I THANK YOU GOD FOR MOST THIS AMAZING/ DAY; FOR THE LEAPING GREENLY SPIRITS OF TREES/ AND BLUE TRUE DREAM OF SKY, AND FOR EVERYTHING/ WHICH IS NATURAL, WHICH IS INFINITE, WHICH IS YES.

—E.E. CUMMINGS

mind and body come together with imagination and skill. Joy is present when our true selves are present, when our love for the glorious nature of our bodies and souls is unconditional. Nothing is seen as an enemy, nothing is hated, annihilated or enslaved. Joy is the gentleness of a child's trusting little hand in our larger one, the rising and setting of the sun, the pure luck of being alive another day.

I FIND ECSTASY IN LIVING; THE MERE ESSENCE OF LIVING IS JOY ENOUGH.
—EMILY DICKINSON

Joy can also be what Susan Griffin calls the search of wholeness, made public. Wholeness carries the memory of what it was like to be a child not yet taught by culture to be divided against ourselves. That place of grace where our breath becomes our link, inside to out, intent to action, heart to heart. Remembering we are all worthy to know love and pleasure. Joy is being captivated by the moment and the will to breathe in this wide and wondrous existence in full safety.

GRACE—THE FIRST AND LAST PRACTICE OF THE WILD.
—GARY SNYDER

Notes

1 *The Practice of The Wild* (New York: North Point Press, 1990), p. 177.

2 Ibid., p. 180.

3 "The Church and Sexual Violence," in *Transforming a Rape Culture*, ed. Buchwald, Fletcher and Roth (Minneapolis: Milkweed Editions, 1994), p. 77.

4 See *The Difference Within: Feminism and Critical Theory*, ed. Meese and Parker (Benjamin North Arm, 1989), p. 9.

5 *Kindness, Clarity and Insight*, trans. and ed. Jeffrey Hopkins (New York: Snow Publications, 1984), p. 60.

6 Ibid., p. 63.

7 Ibid., p. 60.

8 *The Difference Within*, p. 2.

9 *The Dhammapada*, trans. Juan Mascaro (New York, 1973), p. 64.

10 *The Difference Within*, p. 10.

EXERCISES

These exercises are specifically designed so they can be used by individuals, small or large groups. The book and its exercises can be presented in a workshop format and through individual or group study. If using the book at home, the exercises can be explored through keeping a journal or through family discussion after reading the text. In a workshop or study group it would be helpful to distribute the text on the topics before meeting.

A variety of exercises is included. We each have a special way of learning. These ways may be visual, verbal, auditory, tactile, kinesthetic or through writing. Please adapt and interchange the format of the exercises as you see fit. For instance, a journal exercise could easily be changed into a round, or a dyad exercise into concentric circles.

The following is a description of some common forms of exercises. Please refer back to this list if you are planning a workshop or group study and creatively focus the form to your needs.

1. **Writing or keeping a journal**: Writing can be a powerful form of reflecting on ideas and feelings. Through writing, we can deepen self-awareness and bring to light unspoken or unexplored wisdom. It is a safe way of caring for ourselves. The writing guidelines suggested for this work are: (a) there is no right or wrong; (b) there are no rules, especially about spelling or grammar; (c) don't hold back or censor; and (d) your writing always belongs to yourself; share only what you want.

2. **Rounds**: Rounds are helpful ways of sharing ideas in small or large groups. They open the circle for story-telling. In a round, each person has an opportunity to speak without being interrupted. When the person speaking says she or he is finished, there is silence until another speaks or, if going in turn, the next person begins. There is no discussion or cross-

talk until everyone has had the opportunity to speak. Rounds are a positive tool for equal sharing and listening. Successive rounds avoid intellectual debate and the overpowering of the group by stronger speakers. In rounds, each person has the right to pass and is given an opportunity to speak every turn. Rounds are often used in consensus-based groups and healing circles.

3. Dyad/Triad: These are groups of two or three. Participants take turns responding to a question, listening or providing feedback. Dyads and triads are helpful for group-building.

4. Role-play: In role-plays, real or imagined life situations are acted out. Role-plays can be a helpful tool to build confidence, explore alternatives and practice nonviolence. Dramatic simulations can explore aspects of oneself and others in imaginative reworkings of reality.

Reversals or hassle-lines can be a common form of role-play in nonviolence training. Two lines of participants face each other and each line takes a role in a conflict or hassle. Reversals are a fast way of role-playing a number of conflicts and nonviolence techniques.

5. Brainstorm: A brainstorm invites a group to spontaneously respond to an idea or word. It is a form of thinking out loud that can be used with any age group. Brainstorms are used to open up, not to evaluate ideas. This is usually done by writing a word or question on a large piece of paper and asking the group to say as quickly as possible whatever comes into their minds. Each utterance is recorded. One idea usually triggers another and, if not censored, can elicit insightful thoughts. The wilder the better. Rules for brainstorming: (a) say whatever comes to your mind, no matter how apparently irrelevant; (b) don't justify or defend your ideas; and (c) don't judge or discuss the ideas of others.

Clustering is another form of brainstorm. Ideas are spun off through association from a central word or concept, forming a constellation of open-ended exploration.

6. Concentric circles: These work best in large groups. An inner and outer circle is formed with an equal number of facing chairs. Participants speak on a timed topic. At the end of the time the outer circle rotates one space so each circle is now facing a different person. Another topic is introduced, or listening and speaking circles are reversed and the same topic discussed. Concentric circles are a helpful way for participants to get to know each other or to explore an issue with many people in a timed and focused way.

7. **Visualization**: This is imagining in the form of guided fantasies and meditations. Participants are first invited to relax through conscious breathing, quietening or silence. A facilitator guides participants through an imaginary journey or reflection, using verbal cues to provoke imagining appropriate to the work at hand. By yourself, visualizations can be used for relaxation and picturing nonviolent alternatives to situations you wish to change. Try taping visualizations or having a friend read one aloud while you lie down. There are countless ways to use the imagination to create scenes in our minds in which we practice affirming approaches to self and others. For nonviolence to be possible we must first be able to imagine it.

8. **Open sentences**: This exercise can be used alone or with others. Alone, the participant responds to an open sentence by completing it in writing. In dyads, partner A repeats an open sentence given by a facilitator and then completes it with partner B as listener. Partner B stays silent until partner A is finished the sequence. Then roles are reversed. This is an exercise in which we can "hear ourselves into being" with the listener in the role of witness. Create the unfinished sentences with unbiased words that can be easily varied for topics and be truly open to any kind of completion. It is helpful to use a sequence of sentences that progress from views to feelings to responses.

9. **Drawing/collage/clay**: Art is another way of awakening or exploring approaches to nonviolence. As with writing, there is no right or wrong way. Drawing freely with crayons or pastels follows our intuitive sense and can bring out collective or individual images that are important to nonviolent expression. Whether at home or in a workshop, a free drawing or collage can powerfully transmit images that are important to recovery and transformation. Modelling with clay is a wonderful way to gain access to more right-brained (creative) responses to experiences in our lives. Tactile experiences tend to evoke deeper responses. It is important to explore non-verbal expressions that can open different doorways into creative

alternatives. Drawing with your non-dominant hand can also bring different insights.

10. **Games**: It is helpful to utilize games in workshops for their value in play. As adults stricken by the seriousness of life's problems, it is essential that we find ways to experience the joy and playfulness in our lives. There are a number of cross-cultural games that use resources other than language for sharing and team-building. In workshops it helps to use "light and livelies" — fun physical movements and envisioning that don't exclude the comical. Games can encourage crossing over rigid lines and creating new rules where all participants win. Nonviolence, at its best, often uses humor and playful surprise as a way of disarming defences. And most important, play helps us embody our truths physically.

11. **Movement**: Stretching, creative dance, tai chi—any movement that allows energy to open, shift or release. Some of our deepest communication is expressed through the body's non-verbal language.

GROUP GUIDELINES

If you are using this book in a small group the following guidelines are recommended:

1. **Choose a time and place that is consistent**. At the initial meeting, gather together to make introductions, determine group expectations and develop agreements. The topics in the *Our Work* section of this book could be explored weekly for eight weeks, with readings for each topic distributed before each week's meeting.

2. **Rotate facilitation**. Choose a group format that is informal and relaxed yet structured enough to provide a deep focus. People shy to host or guide a meeting need to be supported and given time to develop confidence in the role of facilitator. Communities become stronger when we take this time rather than constantly rely on the same people for leadership. Positive leadership creates independence, not dependence.

3. **Begin with a relaxation or grounding exercise**. This can make a considerable difference to the quality of the meeting. By taking this time an opportunity is provided for participants to truly arrive and be present. Many of us have difficulty relaxing

in healthy ways. Even when we think we are relaxing we may still be distracted and not breathing fully or deeply. Learning often deepens when we relate to each other from a place of calmness, without distraction. Our inability to relax our minds and bodies is widely documented as being an obstruction to health. If not cared for, internal tension eventually finds a release through abuse or illness. Nonviolence begins and ends from a place of calm.

4. **Use check-ins**. They are a way of beginning or evaluating a group process. In a check-in a person says how they are feeling. Check-ins help participants take responsibility for group process and feel more engaged.

At Home

Whether working alone or with others in your family, try to create a space that is conducive to the reflection and sharing this book requires. This can be helped by:

1. Setting a time aside that is planned ahead.
2. Choosing a time when you or your family will not be interrupted.
3. Creating a space that is clear of clutter and visually calming. Arranging comfortable places to sit where (if there are more than yourself) there is good eye contact amongst all family members.
4. Setting a time limit and respecting it.
5. Taking time to relax before beginning. If you are working with the handbook alone or with a few family members, take a few minutes to calm your mind and body by beginning with a moment of silence, by lighting a candle, sitting quietly and breathing deeply, or doing some slow stretches.
6. Checking in with yourself. Write or speak a few words that identify how you are in the present.

Healing Abuse

1. For intensive healing of childhood abuse, Alice Miller's books and J. Konrad Stettbacher's work are excellent resources. Stettbacher's book *Making Sense of Suffering: The Healing Confrontation With Your Own Past* provides a four-step recovery process that can be used with or without the support of a therapist. *The Courage to Heal* by Ellen Bass and Laura Davis

and *Victims No Longer* by Mike Lewis are in-depth workbooks designed for adult female and male survivors of child sexual abuse. Ginny NiCarthy's books *Getting Free: You Can End Abuse and Take Back Your Life* and *The Ones Who Got Away: Women Who Leave Abusive Partners* are excellent resource books for battered and abused women. These books are often available in local bookstores.

2. No one need suffer alone. Consider your right to an informed and supportive therapist who is experienced in abuse recovery.

WORKSHOP FACILITATION GUIDELINES

A whole other book could be written on facilitation. There are many books written about facilitation and group process and much training available for facilitators. For large workshops based on this book, I have summarized the essentials. Please refer outside this book for facilitation information that is more comprehensive.

Understanding the emotional level of the work

Joanna Macy's description of <u>intensive</u> and <u>extensive</u> levels of process work is quite helpful. This description is on page 73 in her book *Despair and Personal Power in the Nuclear Age*. The following summarizes the differences for the purpose of workshop facilitation:

Recovery work can and is meant to provoke powerful emotions that move us past numbness. Extensive forms of work let emotions surface while participants are in control of their expressions. Intensive forms of process work encourage full discharge of emotions in which the participants may require close and skilled support by the facilitator.

Extensive and intensive levels of work overcome different levels of defences and are both ways of moving beyond common resistance to recovery and change. Deeper defences are often the result of past abuses or rigid training. Moving into this level of intensive work with participants can be dangerous if you aren't prepared for the depth of emotion that is released.

This discharge is not necessary for transformation to occur. Transforming our defences into nonviolent action is the result of inner experience that we can touch in countless ways. The most compassionate response we can give to participants working through the topics of this book is one in which we stand beside each other as equals in our efforts and gifts. We are all needed to respect each other's emotions and defences, and we are all needed to engage and to trust in the process.

Facilitation Guidelines

1. Help everyone to participate. Be informed on group process based on equity and mutual sharing.
2. Encourage expression of different viewpoints. Attend to a strong disagreement. Conflicts often yield creative results.
3. Use check-ins and evaluations of exercises and group process.
4. Keep the discussion relevant and focused. Point out when the group is drifting off topic. Acknowledge to the group when people are becoming repetitious or tired.
5. Make sure there are sufficient breaks.
6. Be humble—acknowledge your training or skills as a facilitator as one aspect of who you are. Speak also about your role as a co-learner.
7. Keep your role as a facilitator neutral. If you feel drawn toward a particular position, acknowledge this and ask someone else to step in until the next agenda item. Set aside personal agendas, attachments and ego needs.
8. Remember, all experience is impermanent and non-absolute. Stay fluid.
9. Encourage individuals to pursue strong interests through projects on their own if the group doesn't share the same interest.
10. Use light and livelies and tension-breakers to bring energy into the body and to enliven group process.
11. Use meditation and relaxation exercises to bring calm and focus to group process.
12. Encourage the group to use affirmations and appreciations for the contributions of participants and accomplishments of the group.
13. Stay true to group agreements. For example, begin and end on time.
14. Have food and child care arrangements planned ahead of time.
15. Be committed to the task at hand. This includes being prepared and well rested. Gather necessary art materials, flipchart, markers, paper, pens.

16. Be aware of physical arrangements. Pay attention to creating an environment that is comfortable and inviting. Arrange chairs so eye-contact is possible between all participants. Check lighting and temperature of room.

17. Plan sufficient time for exercises.

18. Have support available before, during and after the workshop.

19. Give an overview of the workshop and goals. Present each day's agenda at the beginning of the day.

20. Be responsive, whenever possible, to the needs of differently abled people. Be sensitive to group members who are illiterate. Be conscious of cultural differences.

21. Help others share their experiences and feelings. Acknowledge and validate contributions.

22. Give and receive feedback.

23. Share your own experiences and feelings. Judge the amount of disclosure helpful to the group.

24. Observe group process and intervene when necessary.

25. Provide time for verbal evaluation of each day's work. Provide time for a written evaluation of the entire workshop.

26. Facilitate a closing exercise that specifically acknowledges closure and future plans.

27. Check out if the group wants names and phone numbers circulated.

28. Have faith in the spiritual process of nonviolent work. Let it be present.

29. Be clear about your intentions behind facilitating.

30. Laugh at yourself and enjoy the work. Bring enthusiasm, curiosity and compassion.

31. Be prepared to be attacked or be used as a lightning rod for feelings evoked through exercises.

32. Appreciate the opportunity to be a fair witness to the profound and simple sharing of participants.

33. Be yourself.

OTHER CONSIDERATIONS IN USING THIS BOOK

1. Approach the readings and exercises with openness. You may find yourself resisting the invitation to explore the ideas presented. If they are new, try not to reject them instantly. When it gets close to home it often feels harder. Sometimes, the part

of us that resists is what needs most attention. Above all, trust yourself and use what you receive in any way you see beneficial.

2. We are all unique. Differences will arise and conflict is inevitable. Conflict doesn't have to be violent. It can be a vehicle for transformation. Watch to see if your agitation is expressed defensively or openly. Often, speaking one's truth without blame and not speaking for another is enough. Remember, there is no one right way.

3. It doesn't matter whether we begin our work with nonviolence by ourselves or with others. Individual and group work are all part of the same circle. If we help ourselves or one person, that is enough.

4. We are all co-learners and co-teachers.

5. Explore, question, be gentle and have fun. All the best on your journey!

NONVIOLENCE EXERCISES

1. Brainstorm or cluster characteristics of violence. Brainstorm or cluster characteristics of nonviolence.

2. Tell/write about a time in your life when an alternative to violence was needed.

3. Make three columns on a large piece of paper with the following headings: power-over/ power-with/ power-within. Brainstorm. Explore the differences. Give real-life examples of each.

4. Round: Take turns telling a story of nonviolence. Include details of the conflict or situation, the participants' roles, and the nonviolent action.

5. Make up a story of a nonviolent response to a real conflict in your life. Write it down. Underline what feels most authentic about your story no matter how idealistic or unimaginable it seems. Do these things.

6. Hassle lines: Think of difficult conflict situations. Each line takes turns playing both sides of the conflict. Consider body language, listening skills, tactics and resolutions used. A helpful variation is to "freeze" role-play and have participants immediately reverse roles in the same situation.

7. What nonviolent campaigns have occurred in your community to counter violence against women and children?

TRUTH AND TESTIMONY EXERCISES

1. In dyads, share an experience of violence in which you were (1) the victim, (2) the violator, and (3) a witness. Each person takes a turn, beginning with the victim, and each ends with a story of being a witness. Take time with each story.
2. How did each experience shape how you respond to violence today?
3. Write/tell about a time you experienced a crisis is your life. How did you get through it? What was the turning point? What support was there? What changed as a result of the crisis?
4. Tell a story about your childhood that is important to who you are today. Begin with the words, *Once upon a time....*
5. Sitting quietly, tell yourself, "my life story is an integral piece of the global quilt." Write about this particular time in your life beginning with the words, *My life today....*
6. Think of a time when you were lied to. Think of a time when you have lied. What were you feeling during those times?
7. Dyad/triad: Do you remember a moment when you were completely in unity with the world? Describe it.*

* from *Life's Companion* by Christina Baldwin

SAFETY AND SANCTUARY EXERCISES

1. What does the word sanctuary conjure for you? Make a list of the feelings, places, sights, smells, textures and sounds that sanctuary represents for you. Write about a real or imagined place in your life that is a sanctuary. Find a comfortable sitting place and imagine for five minutes you are there.
2. Round: Tell about a time you either were given or provided sanctuary.
3. Have pen and paper nearby. Sitting in silence, meditate on the following statement: *My heart is my sanctuary. It can hide and open secrets. It is strong. It is a safe house where unconditional love resides.* After meditating on the above for a minimum of ten minutes, speed write for ten minutes beginning with the words, *Unconditional love....*
4. Write/tell about a time you felt completely in the present without thinking about the past or planning the future.
5. In what ways do you create opportunities for silence in your life? If there is resistance, what is it telling you? What can you

do to provide an environment around you that supports quiet times?

6. Write about a time you spent more than 24 hours alone. How did it benefit you?

7. Round: What sanctuaries exist in your communities? What kind of sanctuaries are needed in your community?

8. Have you ever donated time or money to a shelter for women and children hiding from violence?

DESPAIR AND EMPOWERMENT EXERCISES

1. Dyads: Tell about a time you felt powerless. Tell about a time you felt powerful. How have these experiences shaped how you see the world?

2. Round: What reasons are there for current despair in our lives?

3. Take five minutes of silence. Ask yourself: What might I be grieving for? Share this with someone.

4. Write in a journal about your own definitions of the concepts: (1) despair (2) health (3) transformation (4) love (5) justice

5. If despair were not labelled in your mind with negative connotations, how might you experience it? What do you think would happen if you gave up negative assumptions and let despair take you where it will? What is despair teaching you to pay attention to?*

6. What blessings/gifts can you see coming out of this time?*

7. Tell a story about courage—a time in your life you took a risk.

8. Open sentences:

I think chances for a nonviolent world are getting...

When I think of the world we are going to leave for our children, it looks like...

One of my worst fears is...

The feelings that I carry about this are...

When I try to share these feelings with other people, what usually happens is...

The ways I avoid expressing these feelings are...

The ways I avoid experiencing these feelings are...

*Opening to these feelings I...***

9. Using crayons, paints or pastels, draw an image of personal strength that is derived from your vision of nonviolence. In groups, attach your pictures together with tape. Hang them up. Stand back and wonder about how your personal power

can be deepened by utilizing other forms of nonviolence you see in front of you. Wonder about how your own personal strength contributes to the health of your community. In a round, speak about what you saw.

10. Get up with the dawn. Move for ten minutes, write for ten minutes, sit in silence for ten minutes.

* from *Life's Companion* by Christina Baldwin
** see *Despair and Personal Power in the Nuclear Age* by Joanna Macy

DEFENCE AND DISARMAMENT EXERCISES

1. Ask each of the following questions of yourself. Take your time and write your answers in a journal. Try to go with whatever images first come up for you.

(a) Who are my "beloved enemies"? Who do I identify as the enemies within myself? the enemies outside myself?

(b) What is the form of my inner government? Do I govern myself as a military government? dictatorship? a false democracy? an oligarchy? Is it tyrannical? Is it forgiving?

(c) What warfare do I carry inside? What am I warring against?

(d) What people in my life do I oppress? What parts of myself do I oppress?

(e) Are there slaves in my life?

(f) Am I racist? Am I sexist? Am I classist?

(g) What are my defence systems? What weapons are in my arsenal?

(h) Am I willing to disarm my defences? If yes, my peace treaty will read....

(i) Am I willing to trust or be trustworthy?

(j) Can I learn to tolerate and praise diversity ? Can I develop openness to differences in myself and others?

(k) Can I teach peace to those enemies I carry inside myself?

(l) How can I bring freedom to those aspects of myself that are still in hiding?*

2. There is often at least one monster or burden in our lives. Examples could be addiction, abuse, illness, isolation.... What "monster" is hiding in your family, your community? What is it hungering for?**

3. Identify prejudices against a person or a group that you have now or have had. Where did you learn this prejudice? In what ways do you sometimes behave like the person or group against which you are prejudiced?**

4. Consider: How can I increase acceptance and trust in myself? Visualize yourself in your place of sanctuary. Imagine acceptance and trust each taking the shape of a natural form. Imagine someone you admire presenting these gifts to you. How can you bring acceptance and trust to others?

5. If there were justice for all, what would the world look like? Define what justice means to you. Define what an ethic of care means to you.

6. What gives you courage and insight? These gifts are part of you.

* from *Personal Disarmament: Negotiating with the Inner Government* by Deena Metzger

** from *The Leader As Martial Artist* by Arnold Mindell

ANGER AND ACTION EXERCISES

1. Draw a picture of your anger. Ask your anger what suffering lies beneath it. Ask your anger what it needs. Write the answers in your journal with your non-dominant hand.

2. Open sentence: A way I behave when someone disagrees with me....

3. Journal/Round: How did I experience anger in my childhood and how has that affected the way I express my anger now?

4. What does "think globally, act locally" mean to you?

5. Write/tell about a time you refused to do something because it went against your beliefs.

6. Write about a time you've taken a stand, helped others take a stand. How did you feel and what did you learn?*

7. What action are you ready to take? Who with? What is your intention?

8. What support is there for you from friends, family, community? How can you do what you need to do with joyfulness?*

9. Meditation on breath. Sit quietly. As you breathe in, say silently: "opening." As you breathe out, say silently: "closing." What are you open to? What are you closed to?*

10. Commit yourself to one simple form of nonviolence in the next day.

11. Commit yourself to a nonviolent action with others in the next year.

* from *Life's Companion* by Christina Baldwin

SELF AND OTHER EXERCISES

1. Check-in: The treatment or attitude I most appreciate from others is....
2. Conflict Resolution exercise: (a) Describe a conflict you have in your life right now; (b) Have your friend play the opponent; (c) Take your own side strongly; (d) Notice when you are uncomfortable with your position, have nothing left to say, become neutral, or are taking your opponent's side; (e) Go back to your original role in the conflict and notice if things have changed. Continue through the process until both sides feel they have won.*
3. Think of a woman in your life who you did not or do not value. What was/is she like? How are you like this person?*
4. What "male role" do you reject? Is it possible this role could be incorporated in your life in a useful way? What emotional changes could happen as you imagine this difference?*
5. How would the world change if women were in many of the leadership positions? What gifts would women bring to this work? Which of these gifts could you incorporate in your own work? Whether you are a man or woman, what would happen if you did?*
6. What are your addictions? What are your aversions? How do they keep you isolated? What aspect of yourself have you disowned?
7. Have you ever been an outsider in a group or been treated like an "untouchable?" Have there been times when your group has been prejudiced against others?*
8. Consider:

   The value of friendship and belonging.

   Learning from those people you feel to be most different.

   Taking responsibility for learning about and ending how you discriminate against others who are different in race, sex or class. Taking responsibility for learning and ending how your lifestyle contributes to unhealthy social, economic and spiritual development.
9. Tell/write about a time you wish you had reached out a hand to someone who needed help. Tell/write about a time you have taken a stand and reached out a hand. Consider anonymously giving money to someone in need in your community.

* from *The Leader As Martial Artist* by Arnold Mindell

NONVIOLENCE AND FAMILY EXERCISES

1. Tell a child in your life a story of nonviolence. Invite her/him to make one up.
2. Develop rituals at home that support each others' needs for solitude/quiet times. Give you and your partner opportunity to be alone together, to be comfortable in each other's silence. Arrange times of observed silence when no one in the household talks.
3. Arrange times in your family where you talk in rounds on an agreed subject, all listening carefully without interrupting while each person takes a turn. If the subject brings up a lot, do more than one round. Consider the time this may take as important. If time allows for enough exploration, watch to see if consensus on the subject arises naturally out of the rounds.
4. What kind of world do you want for your children and grandchildren?
   What kind of world do you believe any child deserves?
   What are you doing to make this possible?
5. Using your non-dominant hand, write a letter to the child you once were, at any age. Ask this child to tell you all the things she or he needed but didn't receive. Write these things down. Let this child tell you how he or she was hurt. Write these hurts down. Tell this child what she or he needed to hear and know. Circle the things you still haven't received. Find a way to give yourself these things. Find a way to give these things to the children around you.*
6. Write a letter to a child you know, telling him what peaceful ways of loving you wish for him. Tell her you are happy she was born and why.
7. What is your definition of a family? According to this definition, who is really in your family?
8. Make up or find stories about nonviolence to share with your family. Is there a heritage of nonviolence from your past you can draw from?

* see *Revolution from Within* by Gloria Steinem

NONVIOLENCE AND COMMUNITY EXERCISES

1. What is your definition of community? Of spiritual community? What concerns, beliefs and actions bind and motivate your

community? What diversity of people do you want in your community?*

2. Imagine your ideal nonviolent community. What shared purposes and actions bind and motivate this community?

3. How can you work toward this ideal?

4. In what ways do you sometimes behave like the group against which you are prejudiced? Consider the possibility that this group is an aspect of yourself. How could you use more of this group behavior in your own life? How should you be using less?**

5. What minority groups exist in your community? What are you doing to get to know these people?

6. What commonality do you find in your community? What diversity do you find in your community? How do these commonalities and diversities benefit your life?

7. What is unique about your community?

8. Write a loveletter to your community, appreciating all it has given to you. If you could give anything to your community, what would it be?

9. Sentence completions. I used to assume...

> I still assume...
>
> I used to believe...
>
> I still believe...
>
> I want to believe...
>
> I will...*

10. What does coexistence mean to you? Interdependence?

* from *Life's Companion* by Christina Baldwin
** from *The Leader As Martial Artist* by Arnold Mindell

REFERENCES

Adair, Margo. *Working Inside Out: Tools for Change.* Berkeley: Wingbow Press, 1984.

Adams, Carol J. "I Just Raped My Wife! What Are You Going to Do About It, Pastor?: The Church and Sexual Violence." In *Transforming a Rape Culture.* Edited by Emilie Buchwald, Pamela R. Fletcher and Martha Roth. Minneapolis: Milkweed, 1993.

The Albert Einstein Institute. "Historical Examples of Nonviolent Struggle" and "How Nonviolent Struggle Works." Cambridge, Massachusetts. Mimeograph.

Alternatives to Violence Project, Inc. *Second Level Manual.* New York, 1990.

Altman, Nathaniel. *Ahimsa.* Wheaton: Theosophical Publishing House, 1980.

Amnesty International. *Women in the Front Line: Human Rights Violations Against Women—An Amnesty International Report.* New York: Amnesty International Publication, 1991.

Appleford, Barbara. *Family Violence Review: Prevention and Treatment of Abusive Behavior.* Ottawa: The Correctional Service of Canada, 1989.

Arrien, Angeles. *The Four-Fold Way: Walking the Paths of Warrior, Teacher, Healer and Visionary.* San Francisco: Harper, 1992.

Badgley, Robin et al. *Sexual Offenses Against Children.* Ottawa: Ministry of Supply and Services, 1984.

Baldwin, Christina. *Life's Companion: Journal Writing As a Spiritual Quest.* New York: Bantam Books, 1991.

Biele, Nancy and Peggy Miller. "Twenty Years Later: The Unfinished Revolution." In *Transforming a Rape Culture*. Edited by Buchwald, Fletcher and Roth. Minneapolis: Milkweed, 1993.

Biernbaum, Michael and Joseph Weinberg. "Conversations of Consent: Sexual Intimacy without Sexual Assault." In *Transforming a Rape Culture*. Edited by Buchwald, Fletcher and Roth. Minneapolis: Milkweed, 1993.

Bradshaw, John. *Healing the Shame That Binds You*. Deerfield Beach: Health Communications Inc., 1988.

Buchwald, Emilie. "Raising Girls for the 21st Century." In *Transforming a Rape Culture*. Edited by Buchwald, Fletcher and Roth. Minneapolis: Milkweed, 1993.

Bunch, Charlotte. *Going Public with Our Vision*. Denver: Antelope Publications, 1985.

Butler, Sandra. *Conspiracy of Silence: The Trauma of Incest*. San Francisco: Volcano Press, 1978.

The Church Council on Justice and Corrections and Canadian Council on Social Development. *Family Violence in a Patriarchal Culture*. Ottawa, 1988.

Clark, Suzanne and Kathleen Hulley. "An Interview with Julia Kristeva: Cultural Strangeness and the Subject in Process." *Discourse*, Fall-Winter 1990-1991.

Coomaraswamy, Ananda. *Am I My Brother's Keeper?* New York: Ayer, 1947.

Coover, V., E. Deacon, C. Esser and C. Moore, eds. *The Resource Manual for a Living Revolution*. Philadelphia & Gabriola Island: New Society Publishers, 1977.

Delacoste, F. and F. Newman, eds. *Fight Back: Feminist Resistance to Male Violence*. Minneapolis: Cleis Press, 1981.

Dworkin, Andrea. *Right-Wing Women*. New York: Peregrine Books, 1982.

_____ "I Want a Twenty-Four-Hour Truce During Which There Is No Rape." In *Transforming a Rape Culture*. Edited by Buchwald, Fletcher and Roth. Minneapolis: Milkweed, 1993.

Estés, Clarissa Pinkola. *Women Who Run With the Wolves*. New York: Ballantine Books, 1992.

Federal Bureau of Investigation, United States Department of Justice. *Crime in United States*. 1991, 1992.

Feminism and Nonviolence Study Group and War Resisters International. *Piecing It Together: Feminism and Nonviolence*. London: Co-published by The Feminism and Nonviolence Study Group and War Resisters International, 1983.

Fletcher, Pamela R. "Whose Body Is It, Anyway? Transforming Ourselves to Change a Rape Culture." In *Transforming a Rape Culture*. Edited by Buchwald, Fletcher and Roth, 1993.

Fox, Matthew. *A Spirituality Named Compassion*. San Francisco: Harper & Row, 1990.

Funk, Rus Ervin. *Stopping Rape: A Challenge for Men*. Philadelphia & Gabriola Island: New Society Publishers, 1993.

Gandhi, M.K. *Satyagraha*. Ahmedabad: Nanajivan Publishing House, 1951.

Gioseffi, Daniela, ed. *Women On War: Essential Voices For the Nuclear Age from a Brilliant International Assembly*. New York: Touchstone, 1988.

Green, Tova. "Bundles of Love: Birth of a Social Change Project." *Turning Wheel*, Fall 1993.

Gregg, Richard B. *The Power of Nonviolence*. Ahmedabad: Nanajivan Publishing House, 1949.

Griffin, Susan. *A Chorus of Stones: The Private Life of War*. New York: Doubleday, 1993.

Hahn, Thich Nhat. *Being Peace*. Parallax Press, 1987.

_____ *Interbeing: Commentaries on the Tiep Hien Precepts*. Parallax Press, 1987.

_____ *For a Future to Be Possible: Commentaries on the Five Wonderful Precepts*. Berkeley: Parallax Press, 1993.

Halifax, Joan. *The Fruitful Darkness: Reconnecting with the Body of the Earth*. San Francisco: Harper, 1993.

Harlow, Caroline Wolf. *Female Victims of Violent Crime*. United States Department of Justice, Bureau of Justice Statistics, 1991.

Hedermen, Ed. "Nonviolence." In *War Resisters League Organizer's Manual*. New York: War Resisters League, 1981.

Henderson, Hazel. *The Politics of the Solar Age: Alternatives to Economics*. Indianapolis: Knowledge Systems, 1988.

Hernandez-Avila, Inés. "In Praise of Insubordination, or, What Makes a Good Woman Go Bad?" In *Transforming a Rape Culture*. Edited by Buchwald, Fletcher and Roth. Minneapolis: Milkweed, 1993.

Hill, Steven and Nina Silver. "Civil Rights Antipornography Legislation: Addressing the Harm to Women." In *Transforming a Rape Culture*. Edited by Buchwald, Fletcher and Roth. Minneapolis: Milkweed, 1993.

Hopkins, Jeffrey, ed. and trans. *Kindness, Clarity and Insight: The Fourteenth Dalai Lama*. New York: Snow Lion Publications, 1984.

Hyde, Nadia D. and Helga E. Jacobson. "Still Kissing the Rod: Women and Violence in British Columbia." In *British Columbia Reconsidered: Essays on Women*. Edited by G. Creese and V. Strong-Boag. Vancouver: Press Gang, 1992.

Ingram, Catherine. *In the Footsteps of Gandhi: Conversations with Social Spiritual Activists*. Berkeley: Parallax Press, 1990.

Jones, Anne. *Next Time, She'll Be Dead: Battering and How to Stop It*. Boston: Beacon Press, 1994.

Juno, Andrea and V. Vale, eds. *Angry Women*. A production of *Re/search*, #13, 1991.

Kimmel, Michael S. "Clarence, William, Iron Mike, Tailhook, Senator Packwood, Spur Posse, Magic...and Us." In *Transforming a Rape Culture*. Edited by Buchwald, Fletcher and Roth. Minneapolis: Milkweed, 1993.

Kivel, Paul. *Men's Work*. New York: Ballantine, 1992.

Kornfield, Jack. *A Path with Heart: A Guide Through the Perils and Promises of Spiritual Life*. New York: Bantam Press, 1993.

Kristeva, Julia. *Strangers to Ourselves*. Edited by Leon S. Roudiez. New York: Columbia Press, 1991.

Levine, Stephen. *Healing into Life and Death*. New York: Doubleday, 1986.

Lorde, Audre. *Sister Outsider*. New York: The Crossing Press, 1984.

MacKinnon, Catherine. "Feminism, Marxism, Method and the State: Toward Feminist Jurisprudence." *Signs* Vol. 8, #2 (1983).

MacKinnon, Catherine. "Turning Rape into Pornography: Postmodern Genocide," *MS Magazine, Vol. IV, #1 (July/August, 1993)*.

Macleod, Linda. *Battered But Not Beaten*. Ottawa: Canadian Advisory Council on the Status of Women, 1987.

Macy, Joanna. *Despair and Personal Power in the Nuclear Age*. Philadelphia & Gabriola Island: New Society Publishers, 1983.

_____ *World As Lover, World As Self*. Berkeley: Parallax Press, 1991.

Madhubuti, Haki R. "On Becoming Anti-Rapist." In *Transforming a Rape Culture*. Edited by Buchwald, Fletcher and Roth. Minneapolis: Milkweed, 1993.

Mascaro, Juan. trans. *The Dhammapada*. London: Penguin Books, 1973.

McAllister, Pam. *You Can't Kill the Spirit*. Philadelphia & Gabriola Island: New Society Publishers, 1989.

_____, *This River of Courage: Generations of Women's Resistance and Action*. Philadelphia & Gabriola Island: New Society Publishers, 1981.

_____, ed. *Reweaving the Web of Life: Feminism and Nonviolence*. Philadelphia & Gabriola Island: New Society Publishers, 1982.

Meese E. and A. Parker, eds. *The Difference Within: Feminism and Cultural Theory*. Benjamin North Arm, 1988.

Merton, Thomas. *Gandhi on Non-Violence*. New York: New Directions, 1964.

Metzger, Deena. "Personal Disarmament: Negotiating the Inner Government." *ReVision* Vol. 12, #4, 1990.

Meyerding, Jane, ed. *We Are All Part of One Another: A Barbara Deming Reader*. Philadelphia & Gabriola Island: New Society Publishers, 1984.

Miller, Alice. *For Your Own Good: Hidden Cruelties in Child-Rearing and the Roots of Violence*. New York: Ferrar, Straus & Giroux, 1983.

Mindell, Arnold. *The Leader As Martial Artist: An Introduction to Deep Democracy*. San Francisco: Harper, 1992.

Ministry of Attorney General. *Policy on the Criminal Justice System Response to Violence Against Women and Children*. 1993.

Moore-Foster, W.J. Musa. "Up from Brutality: Freeing Black Communities from Sexual Violence." In *Transforming a Rape Culture*. Edited by Buchwald, Fletcher and Roth. Minneapolis: Milkweed, 1993.

Morgan, Robin. *The Demon Lover: The Sexuality of Terrorism*. New York: W.W. Norton, 1989.

Morton, Nelle. *The Journey is Home*. Boston: Beacon Press, 1985.

Ms. Vol. V, #2 (Sept./Oct. 1994)—special issue on domestic violence.

Murray, Straus and Richard J. Gelles. *How Violent Are American Families? Estimates from the National Resurvey and Other Studies.* 1988.

A National Crime Victimization Survey Report. *Criminal Victimization in the United States.* United States Department of Justice, Bureau of Justice Statistics, 1992.

The National Resource Centre on Child Sexual Abuse. Brochure. Huntsville, Alabama. 1-880-KIDS-006.

NiCarthy, Ginnie. *Getting Free: You Can End Your Abuse and Take Back Your Life.* Seattle: The Seal Press, 1987.

_____ *The Ones That Got Away: Women Who Leave Abusive Partners.* Seattle: The Seal Press, 1987.

Olsen, Tillie. *Silences.* New York: Dell Publishers, 1978.

Peavey, Fran. *By Life's Grace: Musings on the Essence of Social Change.* Philadelphia & Gabriola Island: New Society Publishers, 1994.

Pilgrim, Peace. *Her Life and Work in Her Own Words.* Sante Fe: Ocean Tree Books.

_____ *Steps Toward Inner Peace.* Sante Fe: Ocean Tree Books.

Pitter, Lauren and Alexander Stiglmayer. "Will the World Remember? Can the World Forget?" *Ms.*, April/May 1993.

Plant, Judith, ed. *Healing the Wounds: The Promise of Ecofeminism.* Philadelphia & Gabriola Island: New Society Publishers, 1989.

Ramirez, Rosalinda. In issue, "Love, Justice, Truth, Spirituality" of *Common Ground* Vol. VI (1992).

Reardon, Betty A. *Women and Peace: Feminist Visions of Global Security.* Albany: University of New York Press, 1993.

Rich, Adrienne. *Blood, Bread and Poetry: Selected Prose 1979-1985.* New York: Norton, 1986.

Ross, Jack. *Nonviolence for Elfin Spirits.* Argenta: Argenta Friends Press, 1992.

Russell, Diane E.H. *Rape in Marriage*. New York: Macmillan, 1982.

Schaef, Anne Wilson. *Beyond Therapy, Beyond Science*. New York: Harper Collins, 1992.

Schechter, Susan. *Women and Male Violence: The Visions and Struggles of the Battered Women's Movement*. Boston: South End Press, 1982.

Sheenan, Joanne. "Nonviolence: A Feminist Vision and Strategy." In *Daring to Change: Perspectives on Feminism and Nonviolence*. New York: War Resisters League.

Snyder, Gary. *The Practice of the Wild*. San Francisco: North Point Press, 1990.

Spretnak, Charlene. *States of Grace: The Recovery of Meaning in a Postmodern Age*. San Francisco: Harper, 1991.

Statistics Canada. *The Violence Against Women Survey: Highlights*. Ottawa: Minister Responsible for Statistics Canada, Minister of Industry, Science and Technology, Nov. 1993.

_____ *Stopping The Violence: A Safer Future for BC Women, Fact Sheet No. 2, The Statistics: Violence Against Women in Canada*, Victoria: Ministry of Women's Equality, 1993.

_____ *Wife Assault: The Findings of the National Survey*, Karen Rodgers. Ottawa: Canadian Centre for Justice Statistics, Vol.4, No. 9, 1994.

_____ *Spousal Homicide*, Margo Wilson and Martin Daly. Department of Psychology, McMaster University, Ottawa. Canadian Centre for Justice Statistics, Minister Responsible for Statistics, Vol.14, No.9, 1994.

Steinem, Gloria. *Revolution from Within*. Boston: Little, Brown & Company, 1992.

_____ "Erotica vs. Pornography." In *Transforming a Rape Culture*. Edited by Buchwald, Fletcher and Roth. Minneapolis: Milkweed, 1993.

Stoltenberg, John. "Making Rape an Election Issue." In *Transforming a Rape Culture*. Edited by Buchwald, Fletcher and Roth. Minneapolis: Milkweed, 1993.

Thorne-Finch, Ron. *Ending the Silence: The Origins and Treatment of Male Violence Against Women and Children*. Toronto: University of Toronto Press, 1992.

Walsh, Roger. "Toward a Psychology of Sustainability." In *ReVision*, Fall 1992.

War on Women. A statistical and definitional handout.

War Resisters League. *Handbook for Nonviolent Action*. Co-published by War Resisters League (New York) and Donnelly/Colt (Hampton), 1989.

Worldwatch. Syracuse, N.Y., March/April 1989.

SELECTED READING

NONVIOLENCE

Albrecht, Lisa and Rose M. Brewer, eds. *Bridges of Power: Women's Multicultural Alliances.* New Society Publishers, 1990.

Alpert, David. *People Power: Applying Nonviolence Theory.* New Society Publishers, 1985.

Altman, Nathaniel. *Ahimsa (Dynamic Compassion).* Theosophical Publishing House, 1980.

Bondurant, Joan. *Conquest of Violence: The Gandhian Philosophy of Conflict.* University of California Press, 1969.

Cooney, Robert and Helen Michalowski, eds. *The Power of the People: Active Nonviolence in the United States.* New Society Publishers, 1987.

Fry, Ruth A. *Victories Without Violence.* Liberty Literary Works/ Ocean Tree Books, 1986.

Hahn, Thich Nhat. *Touching Peace.* Parallax Press, 1992.

Hopkins, Jeffrey, trans. and ed. *Kindness, Clarity and Insight: The Fourteenth Dalai Lama.* Snow Lion Publications, 1984.

Ingram, Catherine. *In The Footsteps of Gandhi: Conversations with Spiritual Activists.* Parallax Press, 1990.

Juergensmeyer, Mark. *Fighting Fair: A Non-Violent Strategy for Resolving Everyday Conflicts.* Harper & Row, 1986.

Lakey, George. *Powerful Peacemaking: A Strategy for a Living Revolution.* New Society Publishers, 1987.

Lama, The Dalai. *Worlds in Harmony: Dialogues on Compassionate Action*. Parallax Press, 1992.

Merton, Thomas, ed. *Gandhi on Nonviolence*. New Directions Publishing, 1965.

Patfoort, Pat. *An Introduction to Nonviolence: A Conceptual Framework*. Fellowship of Reconciliation, 1987.

Peavey, Fran. *By Life's Grace: Musings on the Essence of Social Change*. New Society Publishers, 1994.

Peavey, Fran. *Heart Politics*. New Society Publishers, 1986.

Pilgrim, Peace. *Steps Toward Inner Peace*. Ocean Tree Books.

Ross, Jack. *Nonviolence for Elfin Spirits*. Argenta Friends Press, 1992.

Sharp, Gene. *The Role of Power in Nonviolent Struggle*. The Albert Einstein Institution, 1990.

Some Classics:

Freire, Paulo. *Pedagogy of the Oppressed*. Penguin, 1978, 1972.

Gandhi, M.K. *Autobiography: Story of My Experiments with Truth*. Beacon Press, 1957.

Gandhi, M.K. *Nonviolent Resistance (Satyagraha)*. Navajivan Publishing House, 1951.

Gregg, Richard B. *The Power of Non-Violence*. Navajivan Publishing House, 1938.

King, Jr., Martin Luther. *Strength to Love*. Fortress Press, 1963.

Merchant, Caroline. *The Death of Nature: Women, Ecology and the Scientific Revolution*. Harper & Row, 1980.

Tolstoy, Leo. *The Law of Love and the Law of Violence*. Rinehart and Winston, 1970.

Woolf, Virginia. *Three Guineas*. Penguin Books, 1978.

FEMINISM AND NONVIOLENCE

Anzaldua, Gloria, ed. *Making Faces, Making Soul, Hacienda Cara: Creative and Critical Perspectives by Women of Colour.* Aunt Lute Foundation, 1990.

Brock-Utne, Brigit. *Feminist Perspectives on Peace and Peace Education.* Pergamon Press, 1989.

Deming, Barbara. *Revolution and Equilibrium.* Grossman, 1971.

Gioseffi, Daniela, ed. *Women On War: Essential Voices for the Nuclear Age.* Touchstone Books, 1988.

Griffin, Susan. *A Chorus of Stones: The Private Life of War.* Doubleday, 1992.

hooks, bell. Feminist Theory: From Margin to Center. South End Press, 1984.

hooks, bell. *Talking Back: Thinking Feminism, Thinking Black.* South End Press, 1989.

Kimmel, Michael and Thomas Mosmiller, eds. *Against the Tide: Profeminist Men in the United States 1776-1990.* Beacon Press, 1991.

Lorde, Audre. *Sister Outsider: Essays and Speeches.* The Crossing Press Feminist Series, 1984.

McAllister, Pam. *Reweaving the Web of Life: Feminism and Nonviolence.* New Society Publishers, 1983.

McAllister, Pam. *This River of Courage: Generations of Women's Resistance and Action.* New Society Publishers, 1990.

McAllister, Pam. *You Can't Kill the Spirit: Stories of Women and Nonviolent Action.* New Society Publishers, 1988.

Plant, Judith, ed. *Healing the Wounds: The Promise of Ecofeminism.* New Society Publishers, 1989.

Reardon, Betty. *Women and Peace: Feminist Visions on Global Security.* New York University Press, 1993.

Rich, Adrienne. *On Lies, Secrets, and Silences: Selected Prose 1966-1978*. Norton, 1979.

Shiva, Vandana. *Staying Alive: Women, Ecology and Development*. Zed Books, 1988.

Walker, Alice. *Living By the Word*. Harcourt Brace Jovanovich, 1988.

War Resister's League. *Piecing It Together: Feminism and Nonviolence*. 1983.

VIOLENCE AGAINST WOMEN

Abbot, Leslie and John Steitz. *Stop the War Against Women*. Fellowship of Reconciliation, 1990.

Brownmiller, Susan. *Against Our Will: Men, Women and Rape*. Bantam Books, 1975.

Buchwald, Fletcher and Roth, eds. *Transforming a Rape Culture*. Milkweed, 1993.

Bunch, Charlotte and R. Carillo. *Gender Violence: A Development and Human Rights Issue*. Centre for Women's Global Leadership, 1990.

Butler, Sandra. *The Conspiracy of Silence: The Trauma of Incest*. Volcano Press, 1978.

Church Council on Justice and Corrections. *Family Violence in a Patriarchal Culture*. 1988.

Daly, Mary. *Gyn/Ecology: The MetaEthics of Radical Feminism*. Beacon Press, 1978.

Dobash, R. Emerson and Russell P. Dobash. *Violence Against Wives*. The Free Press, 1983.

Dobash, R. Emerson and Russell Dobash. *Violence Against Wives: A Case Against Patriarchy*. Free Press-Macmillan, 1979.

Dobash, R. Emerson and Russell P. Dobash. *Violence and Social Change*. Routeledge, 1992.

French, Marilyn. *The War Against Women.* Summit, 1992.

Griffin, Susan. *Pornography and Silence: Culture's Revenge Against Nature.* Harper & Row, 1981.

Griffin, Susan. *Rape: The Politics of Consciousness.* Harper & Row, 1986.

Guberman, Connie and Margie Wolfe, eds. *No Safe Place: Violence Against Women and Children.* The Women's Press, 1985.

Jones, Anne. *Next Time, She'll Be Dead.* Beacon Press, 1994.

Jones, Anne. *Women Who Kill.* Holt, Reinhart, & Winston, 1980.

Kimmel, Michael, ed. *Men Confront Pornography.* Meridian, 1991.

Kuypers, Joe. *Man's Will to Hurt.* Fernwood, 1992.

Levy, Barrie, ed. *Dating Violence: Young Women in Danger.* Seal Press, 1991.

Martin, Del. *Rape: Battered Wives.* Volcano Press, 1981.

Morgan, Robin. *The Demon Lover: On the Sexuality of Terrorism.* W.W. Norton, 1989.

Pagelow, Mildred Daley. *Woman-Battering: Victims and Their Experiences.* Sage Publications, 1981.

Radforth, Jill and Diana Russell, eds. *Femicide: The Politics of Woman Killing.* Twayne, 1992.

Russell, Diana. *Rape in Marriage.* Macmillan Publishing Co., 1982.

Schechter, Susan. *Women and Male Violence: The Vision and Struggle of the Battered Women's Movement.* South End Press, 1982.

Stanko, Elizabeth. *Intimate Intrusions: Women's Experience of Male Violence.* Unwin Hyman, 1985.

Thorne-Finch, Ron. *Ending The Silence: The Origins and Treatment of Male Violence Against Women.* University of Toronto Press, 1992.

Walker, Gilligan. *Family Violence and the Women's Movement: The Conceptual Practice of Struggle*. University of Toronto Press, 1990.

Walker, Lenore. *The Battered Woman*. Harper & Row, 1979.

RECOVERY AND HEALING

Adair, Margo. *Working Inside Out: Tools for Change*. Wingbow Press, 1984.

Baldwin, Christina. *Life's Companion: Journal Writing As a Spiritual Quest*. Bantam Books, 1991.

Bass, Ellen and Laura Davis. *The Courage to Heal: A Guide for Women Survivor's of Child Sexual Abuse*. Perennial Library, updated 1992 edition.

Bradshaw, John. *HomeComing: Reclaiming and Championing Your Inner Child*. Bantam Books, 1991.

Bridges, William. *Transitions: Making Sense of Life's Changes*. Wesley, 1980.

Cappacchione, Lucia. *The Well-Being Journal: Drawing On Your Inner Power to Heal Yourself*. Newcastle Publishing, 1989.

Davis, Laura. *Allies in Healing: When the Person You Love Was Sexually Abused*. San Francisco: Harper, 1991.

Funk, Rus. *Stopping Rape: A Challenge for Men*. New Society Publishers, 1993.

Herman, Judith. *Trauma and Recovery*. Basic Books, 1992.

Jones, Anne and Susan Schechter. *When Love Goes Wrong: What to Do When You Can't Do Anything Right— Strategies for Women with Controlling Partners*. HarperCollins, 1992.

Katz, Judy. *White Awareness: Handbook for Anti-Racist Training*. University of Oklahoma Press, 1978.

Kivel, Paul. *Men's Work: How to Stop the Violence That Tears Our Lives Apart*. Ballantine, 1992.

Levine, Stephen. *Healing Into Life and Death*. Doubleday, 1987.

Lew, Mike. *Victims No Longer: Men Recovering from Incest and Other Sexual Child Abuse*. Harper & Row, 1992.

Macy, Joanna. *Despair and Personal Power in The Nuclear Age*. New Society Publishers, 1982.

Miller, Alice. *Banished Knowledge: Facing Childhood Injuries*. Doubleday, 1990.

Miller, Alice. *Breaking Down the Walls of Silence*. New York: Dutton, 1991.

NiCarthy, Ginny. *Getting Free: You Can End Abuse and Take Back Your Life*. The Seal Press, 1987.

NiCarthy, Ginny. *The Ones Who Got Away: Women Who Left Abusive Partners*. The Seal Press, 1987.

Paymar, Michael. *Violent No More: Helping Men End Domestic Violence*. Hunter House, 1993.

Sonkin, Daniel and Michael Durphy. *Learning to Live Without Violence: A Handbook for Men*. Volcano Press, 1989.

Steinem, Gloria. *Revolution from Within: A Book on Self-Esteem*. Little, Brown, 1993.

Stettbacher, J. Konrad. *Make Sense of Suffering: The Healing Confrontation With Your Past*. Dutton Penguin Group, 1991.

Stordeur, Richard A. and Richard Stille. *Ending Men's Violence Against Their Partners: One Road to Peace*. Sage Publications, 1989.

Switzer, M'Liss and Katherine Hale. *Called To Account*. Seattle: Seal Press, 1987.

Travis, Carol. *Anger: The Misunderstood Emotion*. Simon & Shuster, 1982.

Welwood, John. *Journey of the Heart: Intimate Relationship and the Path of Love*. Harper Collins, 1981.

MEDITATION AND SPIRITUALITY

Cooper, David. *Silence, Simplicity and Solitude: A Guide for Spiritual Retreat*. Bell Tower/Crown, 1992.

Feldman, Christina and Jack Kornfield, eds. *Stories of the Spirit, Stories of the Heart: Parables of the Spiritual Path from Around the World*. San Francisco: Harper, 1992.

Goldstein, Joseph. *The Experience of Insight: A Simple and Direct Guide to Buddhist Meditation*. Shambhala, 1987.

Hahn, Thich Nhat. *Being Peace*. Parallax Press, 1987.

Hahn, Thich Nhat. *Present Moment, Wonderful Moment: Mindfulness Verses for Daily Living*. Parallax Press, 1984.

Hirshfield, Jane, ed. *Women in Praise of the Sacred: 43 Centuries of Spiritual Poetry by Women*. HarperCollins, 1994.

Kelly, Marcia and Jack Kelly, eds. *One Hundred Graces*. Bell Tower/Crown, 1992.

Levine, Stephen. *Guided Meditations, Explorations and Healings*. Doubleday, 1991.

Miller, Ronald and eds., *As Above, So Below: Paths to Spiritual Renewal In Daily Life*. Tarcher/Putman, 1992.

Mitchell, Stephen, ed. *The Enlightened Heart: An Anthology of Sacred Poetry*. HarperCollins, 1989.

Moore, Thomas. *Care of the Soul: A Guide For Cultivating Depth and Sacredness in Everyday Living*. HarperCollins, 1992.

Moyne, John and Coleman Barks, trans. *Open Secret: Versions of Rumi*. Threshold Books, 1984.

Packer, Toni. *The Work of This Moment*. Shambhala, 1991.

The Path of the Heart: A Guide Through the Perils and Promises of Spiritual Life. Bantam Books, 1993.

SERVICE

Coover et al., eds. *Resource Manual for a Living Revolution: A Handbook of Skills and Tools for Social Change Activities*. New Society Publishers, 1977.

Dass, Ram and Maribai Bush. *Compassion in Action: Setting Out On the Path of Service*. Bell Tower/Crown, 1992.

Dass, Ram and Paul Gorman. *How Can I Help? Stories and Reflections on Service*. Alfred A. Knopf Inc. 1985.

Elgin, Duane. *Voluntary Simplicity: Toward a Way of Life that is Outwardly Simple, Inwardly Rich*. William Morrow & Company, 1981.

Eppsteiner, Fred, ed. *The Path of Compassion: Writings on Socially Engaged Buddhism*. Parallax Press, 1988.

Green, Tova and Peter Woodrow with Fran Peavey. *Insight and Action: How to Discover and Support a Life of Integrity and Commitment to Change*. New Society Publishers, 1994.

The Centre for Conflict Resolution. *Building United Judgement: A Handbook for Consensus Decision-Making*. New Society Publishers, 1981.

CHILDREN AND FAMILY

Berends, Polly B. *Gently Lead: How to Teach Your Child About God While Finding Out for Yourself*. HarperCollins, 1991.

Carlsson-Paige, Nancy and Diane E. Levin. *Who's Calling the Shots: How to Respond Effectively to Children's Fascination with War Play and War Toys*. New Society Publishers, 1990.

Crary, Elizabeth. *Kids Can Cooperate: A Practical Guide to Teaching Problem Solving*. Parenting Press, 1984.

Creighton, Allan and Paul Kivel. *A Practical Guide for Parents, Counsellors and Educators Helping Teens Stop Violence*. Oakland Men's Project and Battered Women's Alternatives, 1990.

Daley, Dennis and Janet Sinburg. *I Can Talk About What Hurts: A Book for Kids in Homes Where There's Chemical Dependency.* Hazelden, 1989.

Dorn, Lois. *Peace in the Family: A Workbook of Ideas and Actions.* Pantheon Books, 1985.

Grasso, Jean. *Something More: Nurturing Your Child's Spiritual Growth.* Fitzpatrick, Penguin, 1992.

Haessly, Jacqueline. *PeaceMaking: Family Activities for Justice and Peace.* Paulist Press, 1980.

Mander, Jerry. *Four Arguments for the Elimination of Television.* Quill, 1978.

McGinnis, Kathleen and Barbara Oehlberg. *Starting Out Right: Nurturing Young Children as PeaceMakers.* New Society Publishers, 1988.

Mildzan, Myriam. *Boys Will be Boys: Breaking the Link Between Masculinity and Violence.* Doubleday, 1992.

Miller, Alice. *Thou Shalt Not Be Aware: Society's Betrayal of the Child.* Farrar, Straus & Giroux, 1984.

Prutzman, Priscilla et al. *The Friendly Classroom for a Small Planet: A Handbook on Creative Approaches to Living and Problem Solving for Children.* New Society Publishers, 1988.

Wichert, Susanne. *Keeping the Peace: Practising Cooperation and Conflict Resolution with Preschoolers.* New Society Publishers, 1989.

One of the best annotated bibliographies available for written materials on CHILD SEXUAL ABUSE EDUCATION, PREVENTION AND TREATMENT is available through Siecus' Publication Department, 130 West 42nd Street, Suite 2500, New York, NY 10036; 212/819-9770, fax 212/819-9776.

TRANSFORMATION AND VISION

Arrien, Angeles. *The Four-Fold Way: Walking the Path of the Warrior, Teacher, Healer and Visionary.* San Francisco: Harper, 1992.

Eisler, Riane. *The Chalice and the Blade.* Harper & Row, 1987.

Forsey, Helen, ed. *Circles of Strength: Community Alternatives to Alienation.* New Society Publishers, 1992.

Griffin, Susan. *Made From This Earth: An Anthology of Writings.* The Women's Press, 1982.

Hahn, Thich Nhat. *For a Future to be Possible: Commentaries on the Five Wonderful Precepts.* Parallax Press, 1993.

Halifax, Joan. *The Fruitful Darkness: Reconnecting with the Body of the Earth.* Harper Collins, 1994.

Henderson, Hazel. *Paradigms in Progress: Life Beyond Economics.* Knowledge Systems, 1992.

LaChapelle, Delores. *Sacred Land, Sacred Sex, Rapture of the Deep: Concerning Deep Ecology and Celebrating Life.* Finn Hill Arts, 1988.

Macy, Joanna. *World As Lover, World As Self.* Parallax Press, 1991.

Mander, Jerry. *In the Absence of the Sacred: The Failure of Technology and the Survival of the Indian Nations.* Sierra Club, 1991.

Mindell, Arnold. *The Leader As Martial Artist: Techniques and Strategies for Resolving Conflict and Creating Community.* San Francisco: Harper, 1992.

Rich, Adrienne. *What is Found There: Notebooks on Poetry and Politics.* Norton, 1993.

Sams, Jamie. *The 13 Original Clan Mothers.* HarperCollins, 1993.

Spangler, David and William Irwin. *Reimagination of the World: A Critique of the New Age, Science and Popular Culture.* Bear & Co., 1991.

Spretnak, Charlene. *States of Grace: The Recovery of Meaning in the Postmodern Age.* HarperCollins, 1991.

Starhawk, *Truth or Dare: Encounters with Power, Authority and Mystery.* Harper & Row, 1989.

Ywahoo, Dhyani. *Voice of Our Ancestors: Cherokee Teachings from the Wisdom Fire.* Shambhala, 1987.

NEW SOCIETY PUBLISHERS

New Society Publishers is a not-for-profit, worker-controlled publishing house. We are proud to be the only publishing house in North America committed to fundamental social change through nonviolent action.

We are connected to a growing worldwide network of peace, feminist, religious, environmental, and human rights activists, of which we are an active part. We are proud to offer powerful nonviolent alternatives to the harsh and violent industrial and social systems in which we all participate. And we deeply appreciate that so many of you look to us for resources in these challenging and promising times.

New Society Publishers is a project of the New Society Educational Foundation in the U.S., and the Catalyst Education Society in Canada. We are not the subsidiary of any transnational corporation; we are not beholden to any other organization; and we have neither stockholders nor owners in any traditional business sense. We hold this publishing house in trust for you, our readers and supporters, and we appreciate your contributions and feedback.

NSP publishes a number of books that complement this one. For a full catalogue, contact us at one of the addresses below:

In Canada:

P.O. Box 189,
Gabriola Island, BC
Canada V0R 1X0

In the U.S.A.:

4527 Springfield Avenue,
Philadelphia, PA
USA 19143

4035